PUT A MONOCLE ON IT

A Collection of Critters with Style and Personality

BY
TAMI BOYCE

Copyright © 2017 Tami Boyce
All rights reserved.

Edited by Susan Burlingame
www.sites.google.com/site/sjbwords1

ISBN: 0692995390
ISBN-13: 978-0692995396

Tami Boyce Design
Charleston, South Carolina

*To everyone who has supported the Monocle Series since it's conception.
You gave me the voice and confidence to seek out my fellow weirdos.
For that, I can never thank you enough.*

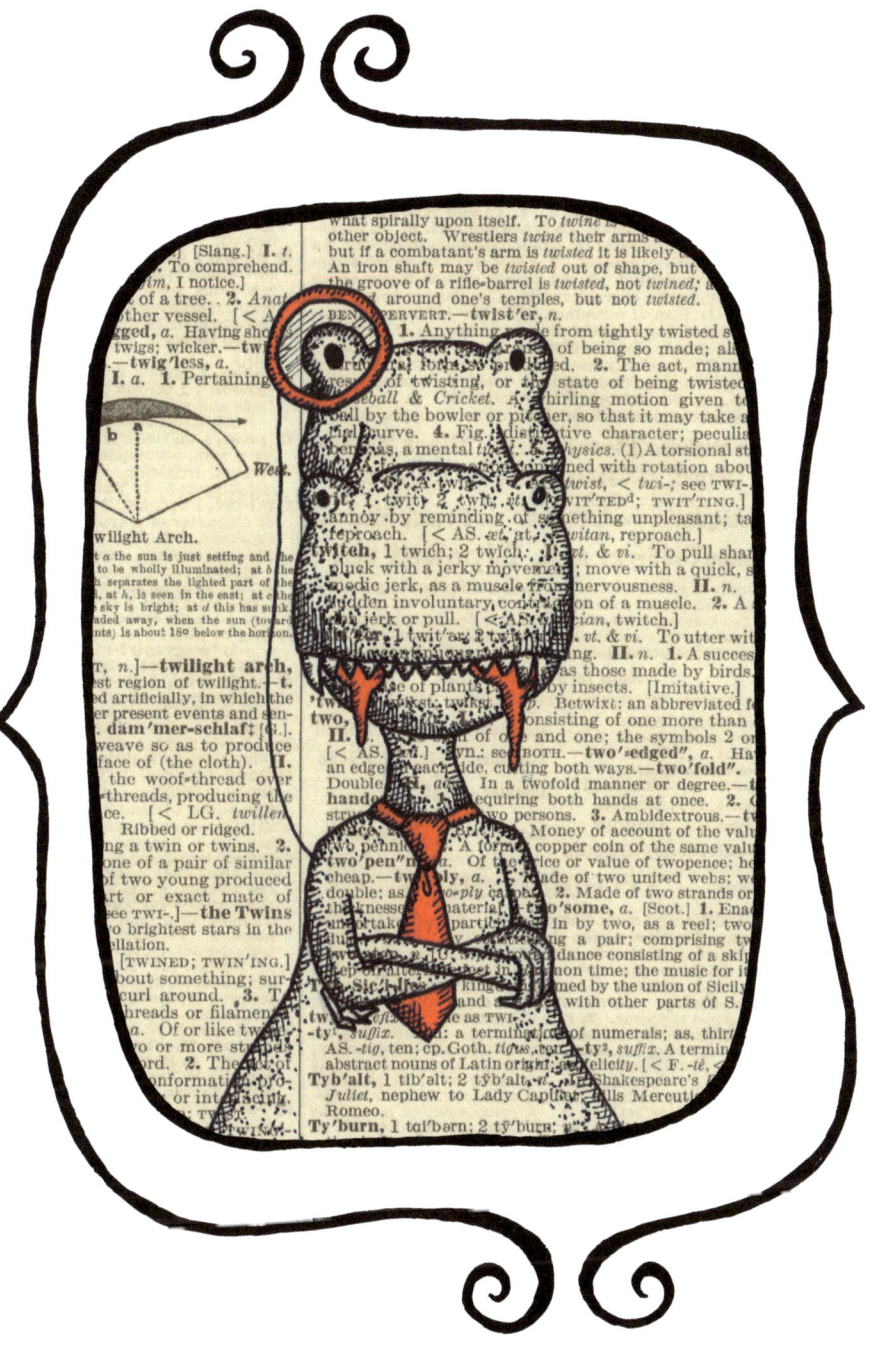

Meet Ned the T-Rex

Ned the T-Rex was pretty much into fashion before it was even invented. And really, what could ever accent a little blood on the face better than a Windsor knot below it? In a word, Ned is just "timeless."

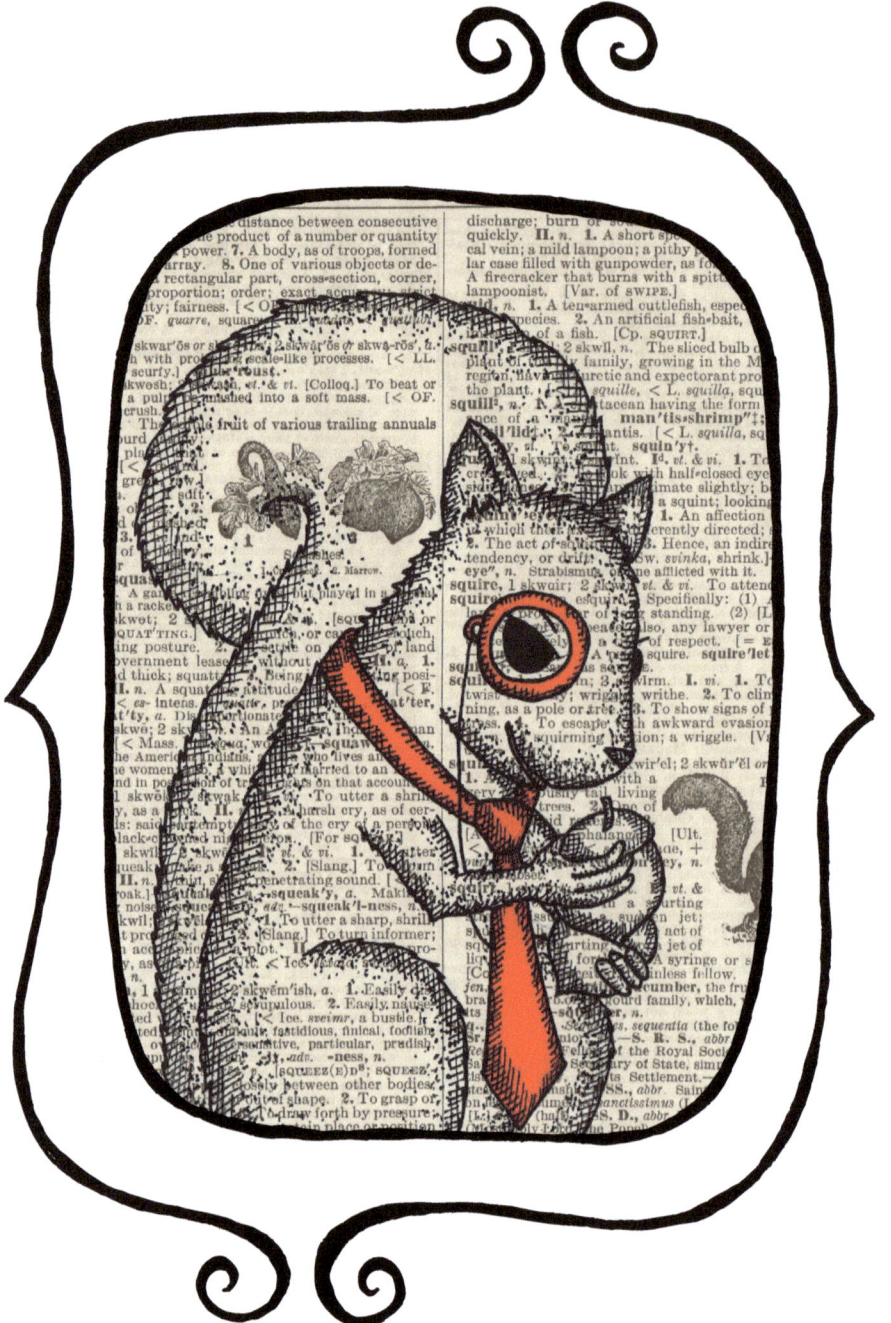

Meet Bradley the Squirrel

Don't let Bradley's fluffy, adorable appearance fool you. He may be one of the cutest creatures on the planet, but he's also one of the deadliest. Challenge Bradley on a bad day, and you might wake up with rabies. Engage Bradley in a pleasant and inviting way, and you might find he is willing to share his highly sought-after nut collection.

Meet Reginald the Platypus

Reginald's mantra is, "Why swim when we can just take the yacht?" Though he wouldn't classify himself as an elitist or snob, Reginald believes that when you possess both personality and charisma, you're just naturally better than most people.

Meet Cyril the Lion

Cyril was captain of the debate team, a gold medalist in the 2008 Animal Olympics, and an extraordinary nap-taker. With a résumé like his, not to mention his regally manicured beard, it's no wonder Cyril is the uncontested king of the jungle.

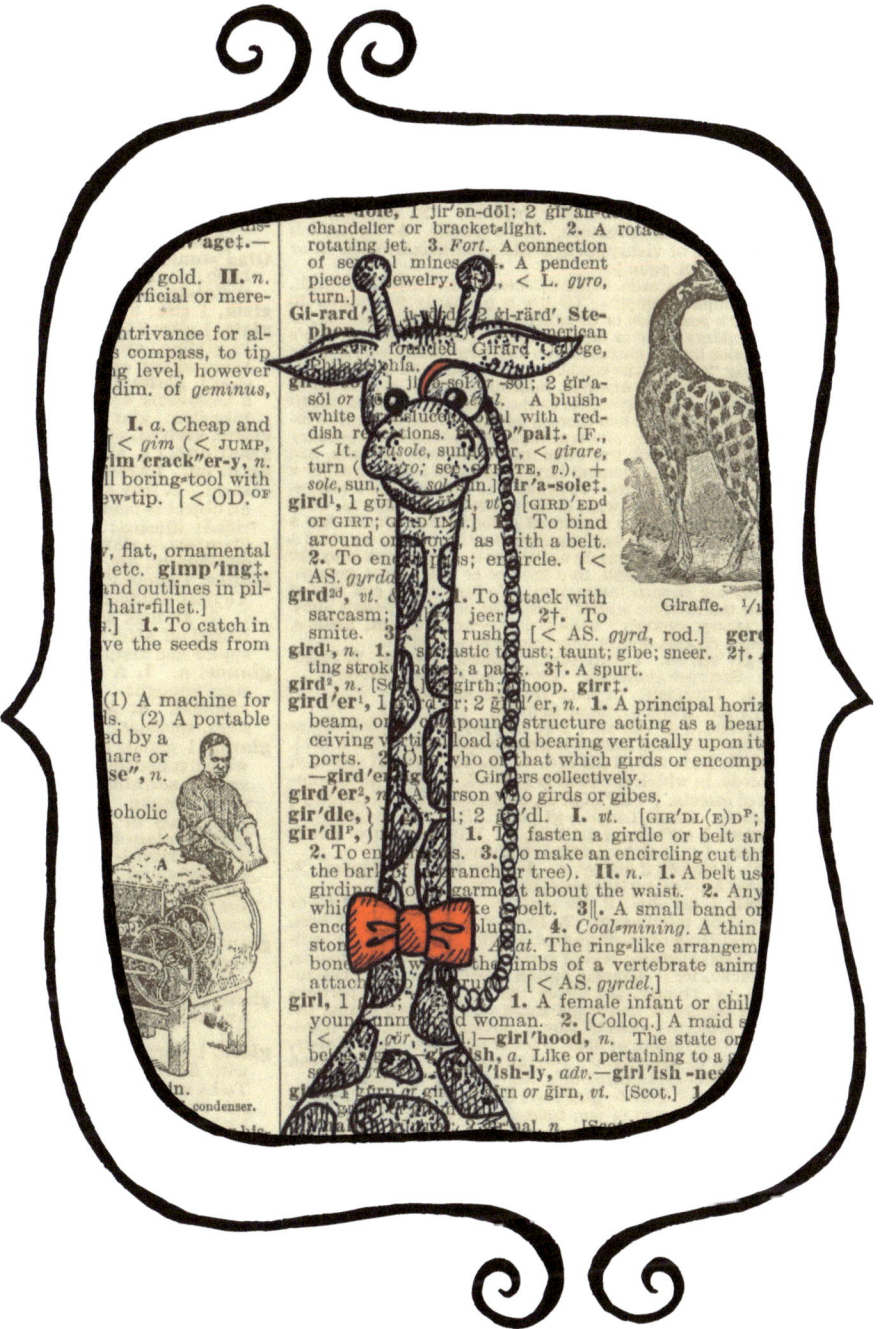

Meet Lloyd the Giraffe

Never making an appearance without looking dapper, Lloyd is also one of the funniest and kindest souls you'll ever meet. When it comes to work, he's never afraid to get his hooves dirty, but he does it with effortless style. If you're ever in the Savannah, I highly recommend eating some leaves with this guy.

Meet Higgins the Owl

How many licks does it take to get to the center of a Tootsie Pop? Higgins believes the world would know had it asked a smarter owl. Higgins is highly respected among his fellow owls, but he doesn't flaunt his intelligence. He'd rather just be left alone to quietly revel in it. In fact, Higgins's favorite joke is, "How do you know someone has a master's degree in English? Don't worry…they'll tell you."

Meet Lorenzo the Llama

Lorenzo is quite the sassy, yet charming, world traveler! Besides the few times he has been found spitting in inappropriate places, he is usually well-received on his travels. Should you ever have the pleasure of meeting the suave Lorenzo, put your hand over your glass and let the good times roll.

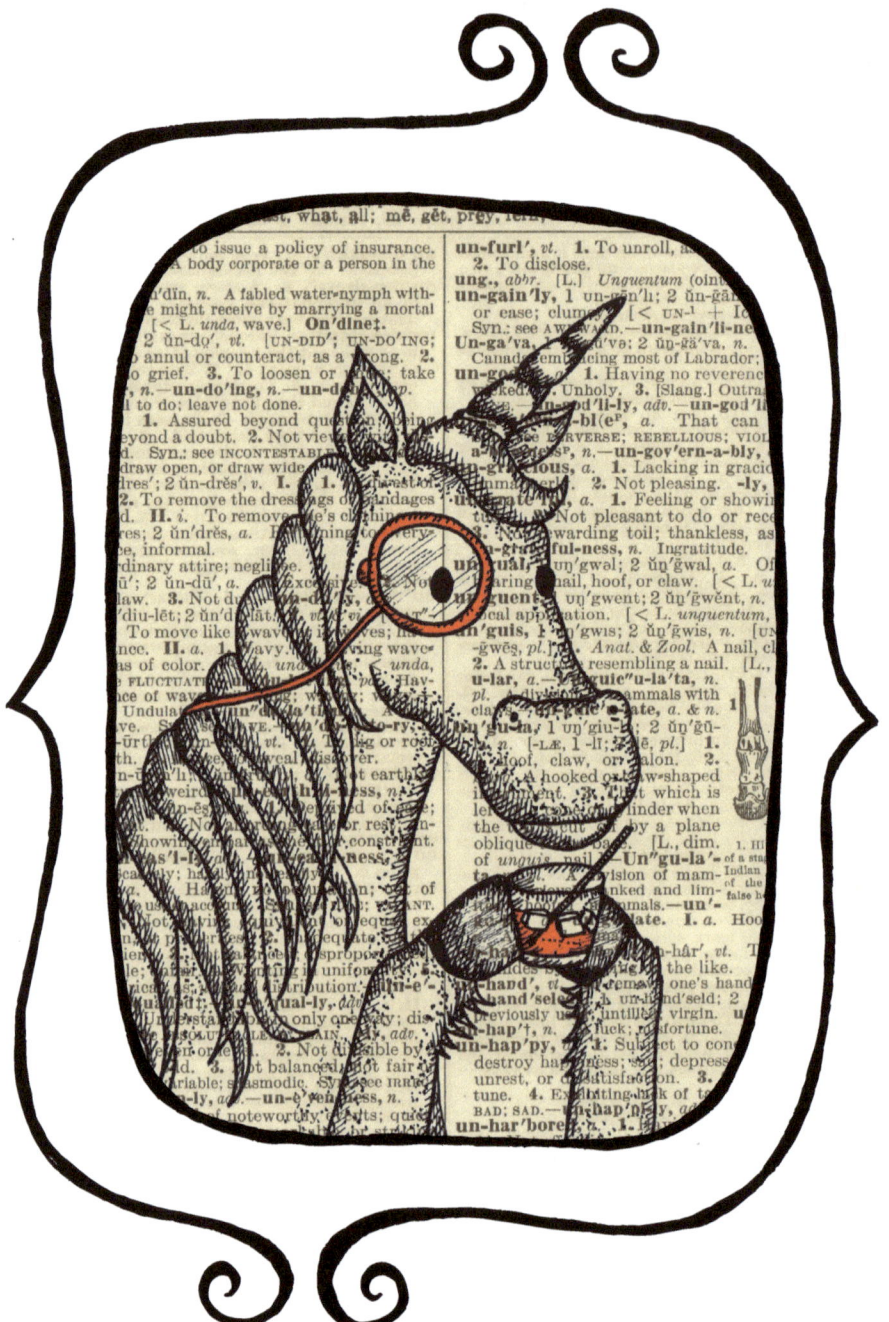

Meet Ernest the Unicorn

Ernest is a trail-blazing and trend-setting unicorn. He knows that unicorn life isn't just about rainbows and magic, as he proudly sips his high-end cocktails. Is Ernest simultaneously defying the squeaky-clean, Lisa Frank stereotype while ignoring judgmental looks he may receive? Of course! Because he's a mother friggin' unicorn.

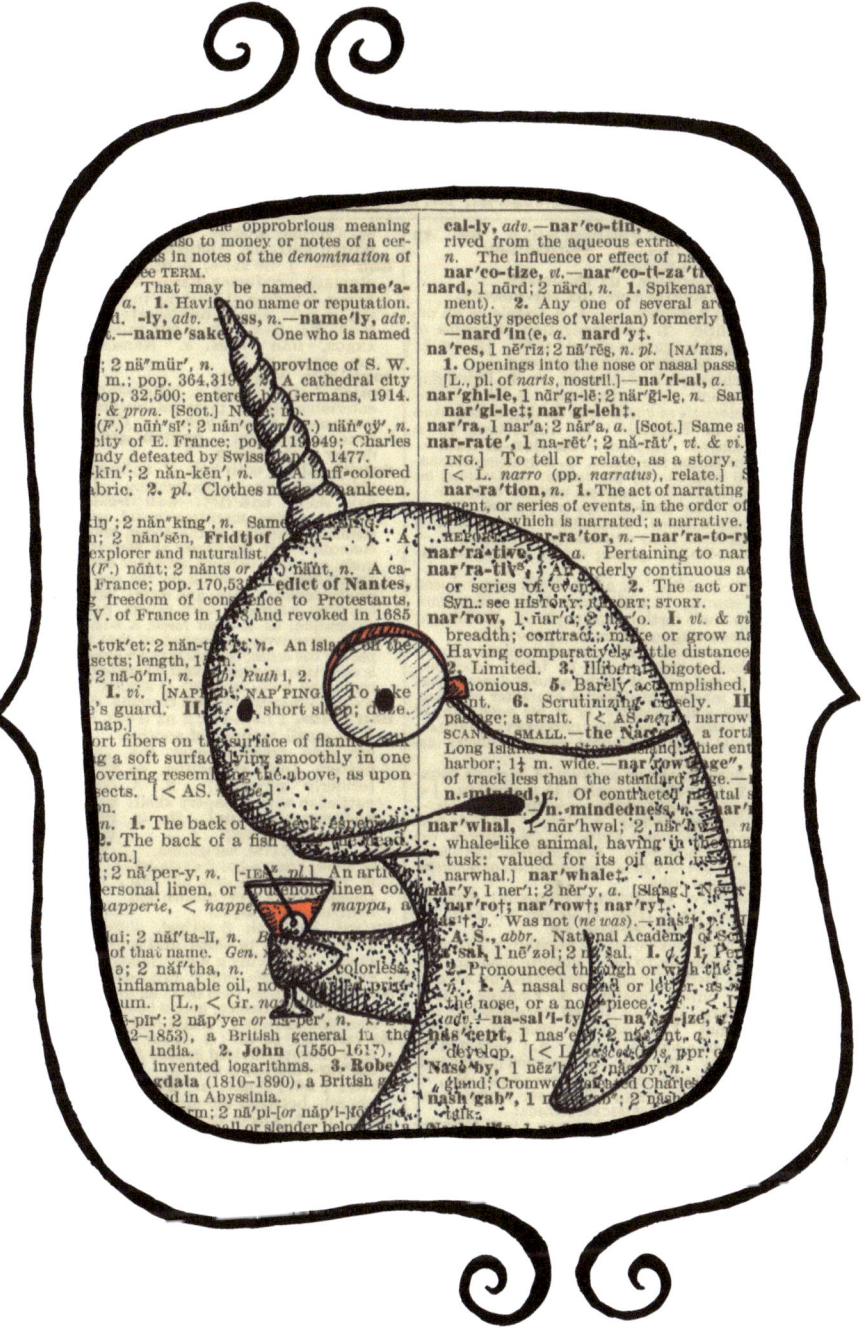

Meet Mort the Narwhal

Though Mort is the type that can usually be found grumbling in the corner at parties, he has an undeniable charisma about him. It's probably because the negative things Mort says are usually true…and always entertaining. The sarcastic duo of Mort and Ernest the Unicorn is pure magic!

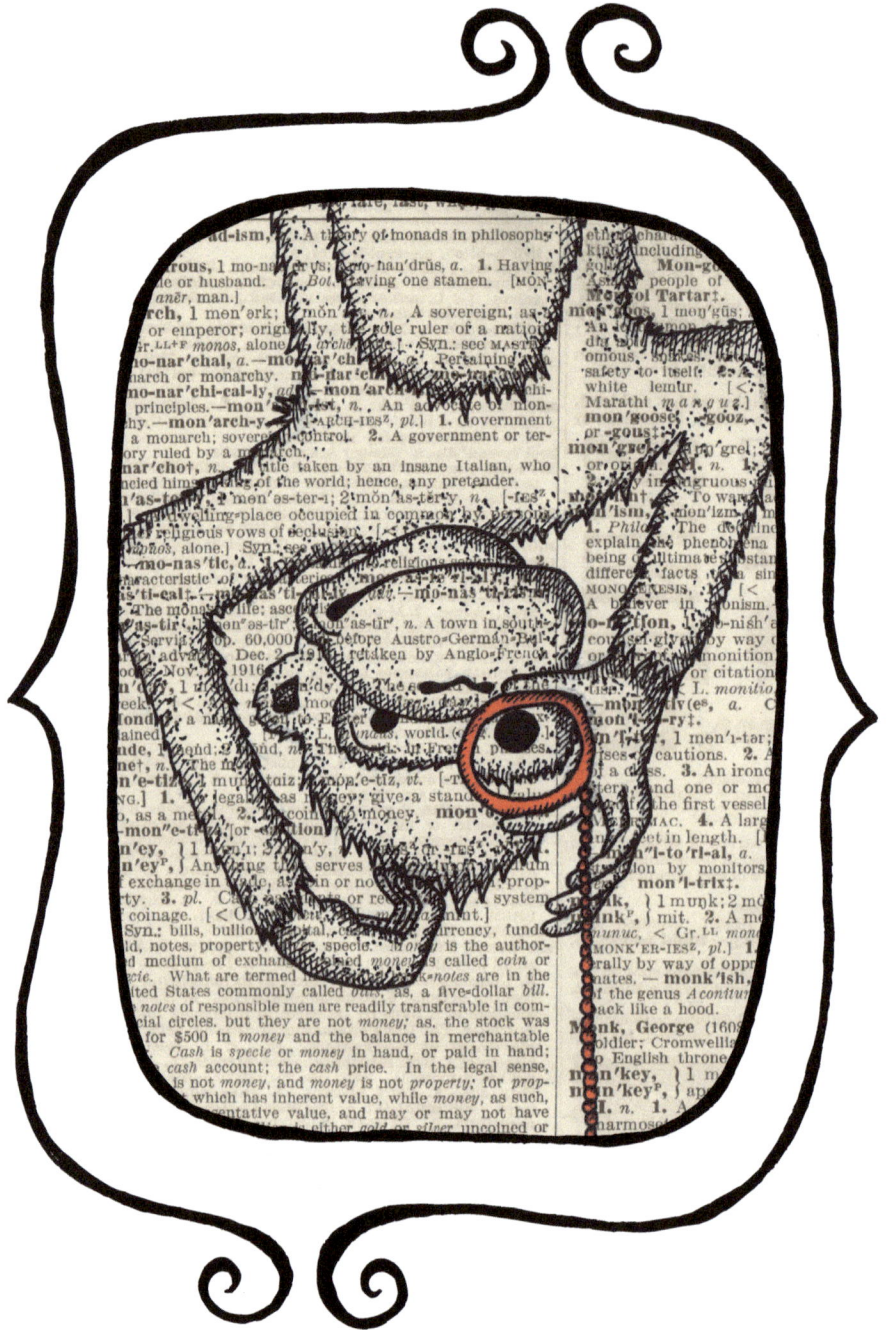

Meet Virgil the Monkey

Virgil is living proof that someone can be intelligent, high-brow, AND fun-loving. He's mastered sign language and flight simulation, and he loves 90% of all Kevin Smith movies. After following many U.S. presidential campaigns, Virgil is considering a future in politics and feels quite confident about his chances.

Meet Bernard the Tortoise

Ever wonder why tortoises are so slow? Nature's secret: they are stoned out of their minds. The truth is, most tortoises are high-functioning potheads who carry their houses on their backs in case they forget their address. Bernard is a huge fan of philosophy, poetry, and cheese doodles.

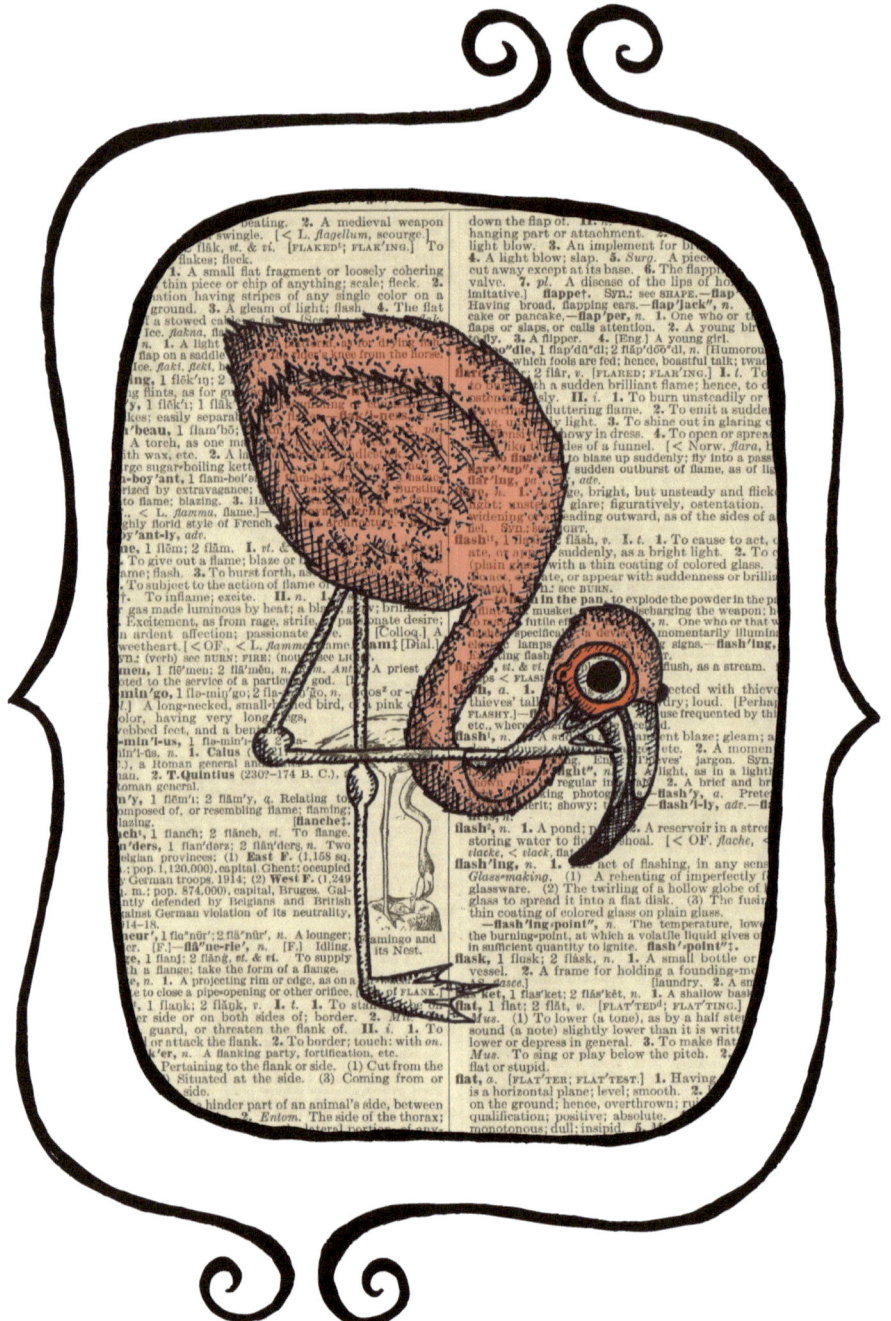

Meet Harold the Flamingo

Harold is one opinionated bird. He has firm thoughts on politics, seafood, and a guy's intrinsic right to wear pink. When you are in the company of Harold, it is probably best not to make a wise crack about "tacky" yard flamingos. His well-versed rant does make a good point: "Out of all the tacky things one can find in a typical Floridian home, pink flamingos aren't even on the radar."

Meet Sam the Alligator

Who's got time for the tears of a crocodile when you're the happiest alligator in the world? And because of his radiant positivity, Sam does a lot to displace the negative qualities associated with his kind. When Sam's not swimming on the Bayou, he enjoys sinking his teeth into a good book or volunteering at local albino alligator shelters.

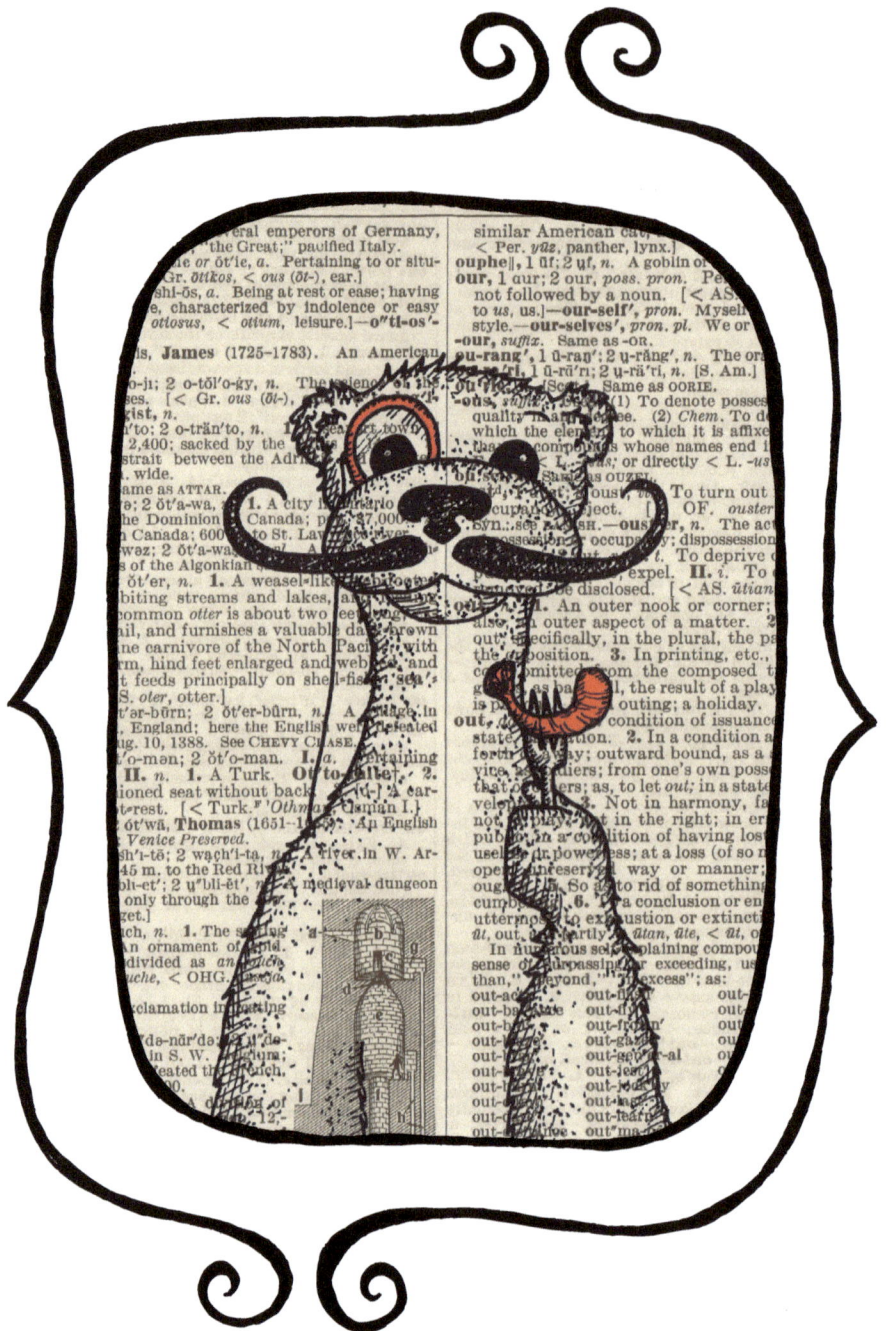

Meet Lewis the Otter

If you want Lewis to come to your party, tell him there will be free food. If you want Lewis to help you move a couch—good luck. He may not be your most reliable friend, but the mustache and charm will surely elevate Lewis as one of your favorites.

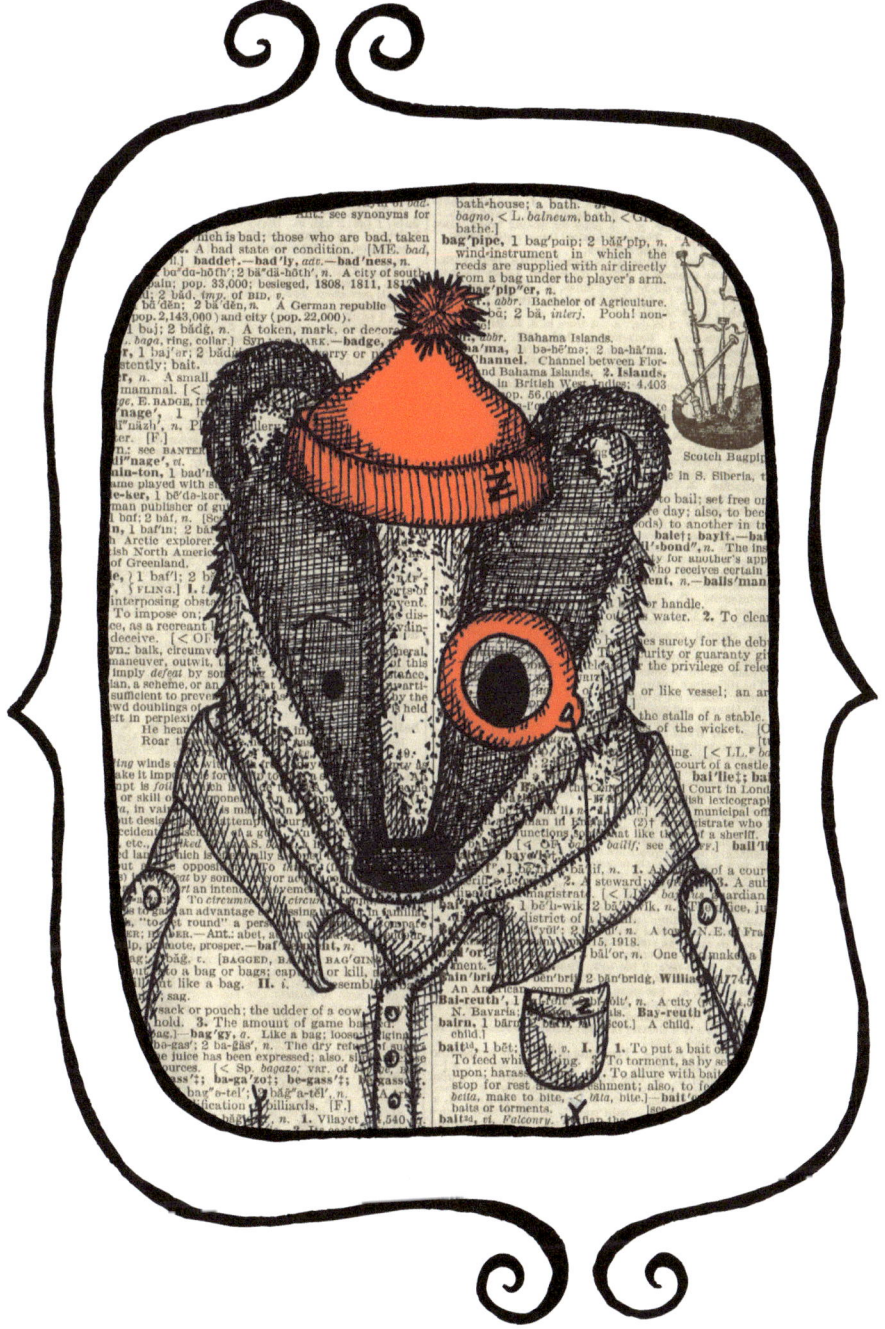

Meet Davey the Badger

Davey doesn't mean to be a liar, he's just one of those creatures who doesn't let the truth get in the way of a good story. A huge Bill Murray fan, Davey will inevitably tell you that the badger character from *Fantastic Mr. Fox* is based on him. It's best to just sit back, enjoy the tale, and give Davey a break. What else do badgers really have to brag about?

Meet Leonard the Sloth

True to his sloth culture, Leonard does not live life in the fast lane. But when you are loyal, fabulous, and adorable, who cares if you're in the slow lane? Of course, Leonard's "slow lane" is actually more like the road's emergency shoulder. If you make a date with Leonard, it's best to clear your schedule for the next day or two.

Meet Jinx the Fox

As a high-end bartender, Jinx serves a stout 1:1 ratio of sarcasm to drinks. And while he may not be the fastest or best bartender around, Jinx knows that with a face like his, he doesn't have to be.

Meet Vince the Pig

Vince is a nice enough guy. He's also the kind of friend you invite over for dinner and realize two weeks later that he is still living at your house. You learn to forgive Vince because his stories are unforgettable and his heart is mostly in the right place. Despite his propensity for raiding the refrigerator and overstaying his welcome, Vince really is "some pig."

Meet General Sawyer the Rooster

What embodies the American dream more than a rooster in a three piece suit? General Sawyer is a self-made fowl who ascended through the ranks with hard work and determination. While in his company, if you ever comment about the similar uniforms of General Sawyer and Colonel Sanders, prepare to see a few ruffled feathers.

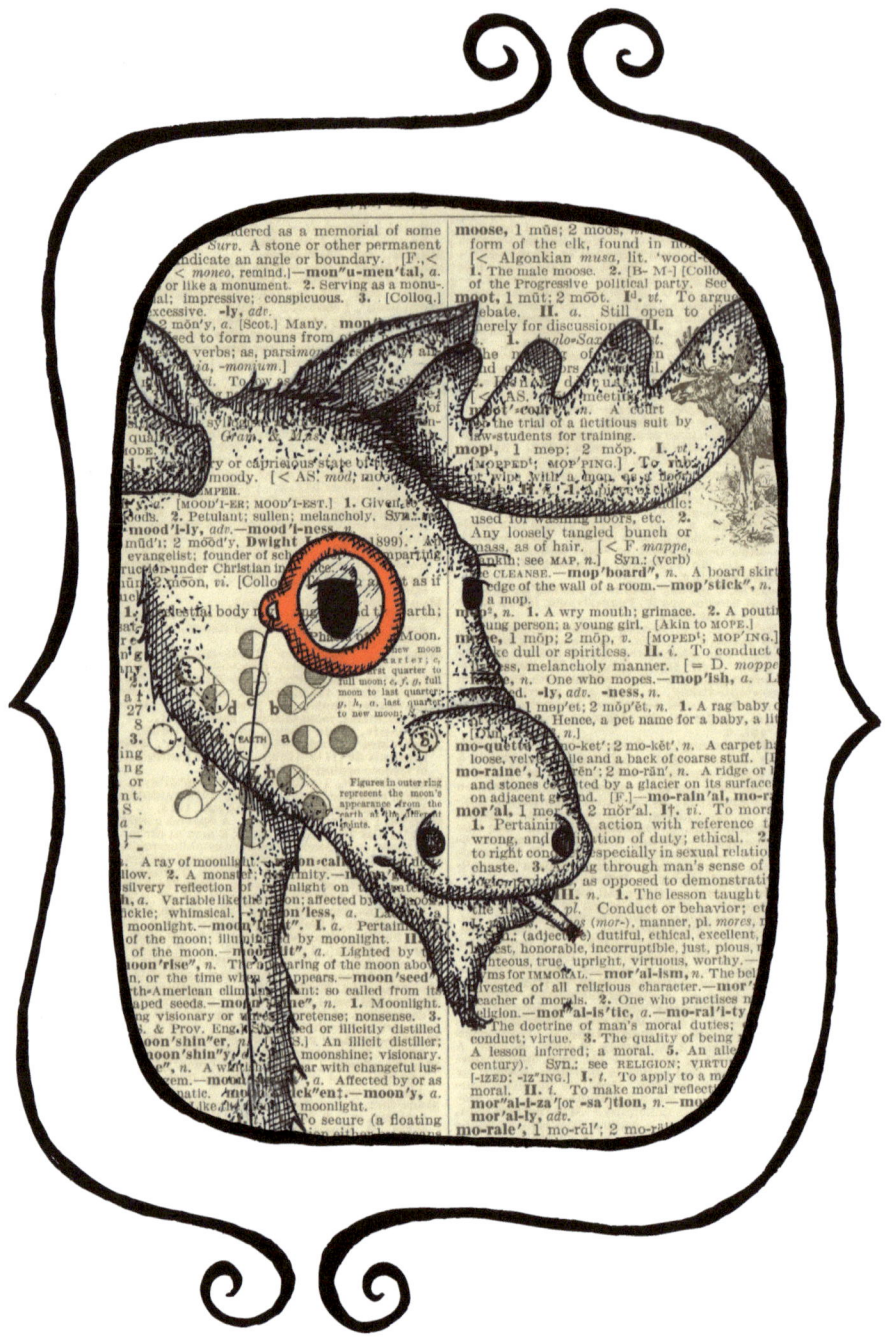

Meet Dash the Moose

Dash is a true bad-ass. Imagine James Dean and Fonzie morphed into one moose's body. Dash turns being an aloof heartthrob into an art form. Needless to say, he doesn't have a whole lot of free time once mating season hits.

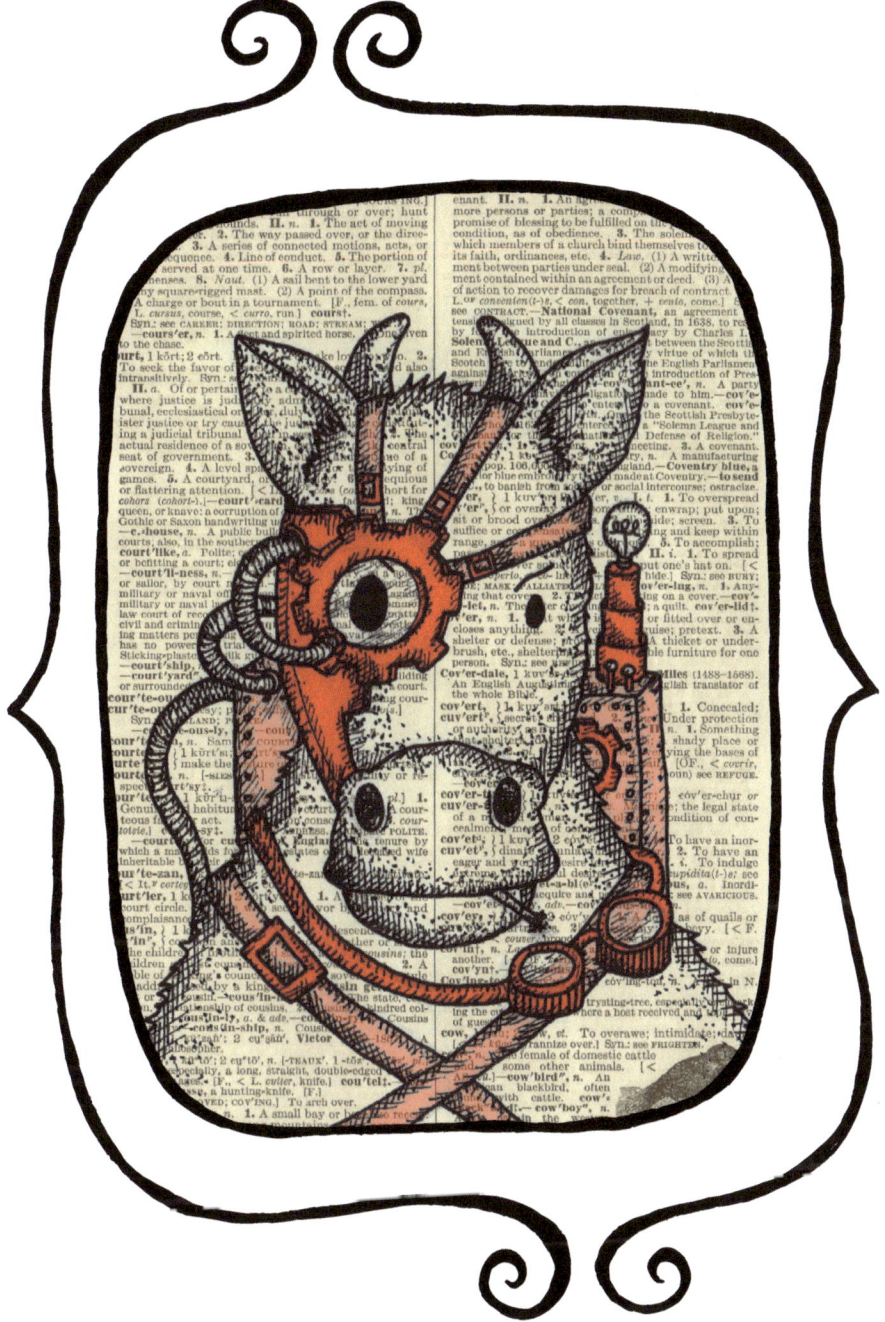

Meet Lucius the Cow

Lucius is one intense bovine. His borderline-unhealthy obsession with steampunk culture and the *Mad Max* movies makes Lucius walk that tightrope between being fascinating and being crazy. Of course, should the "inevitable" apocalypse happen, Lucius is a handy friend to have. His secret stockpiles make the people on *Doomsday Preppers* look like they're planning a picnic.

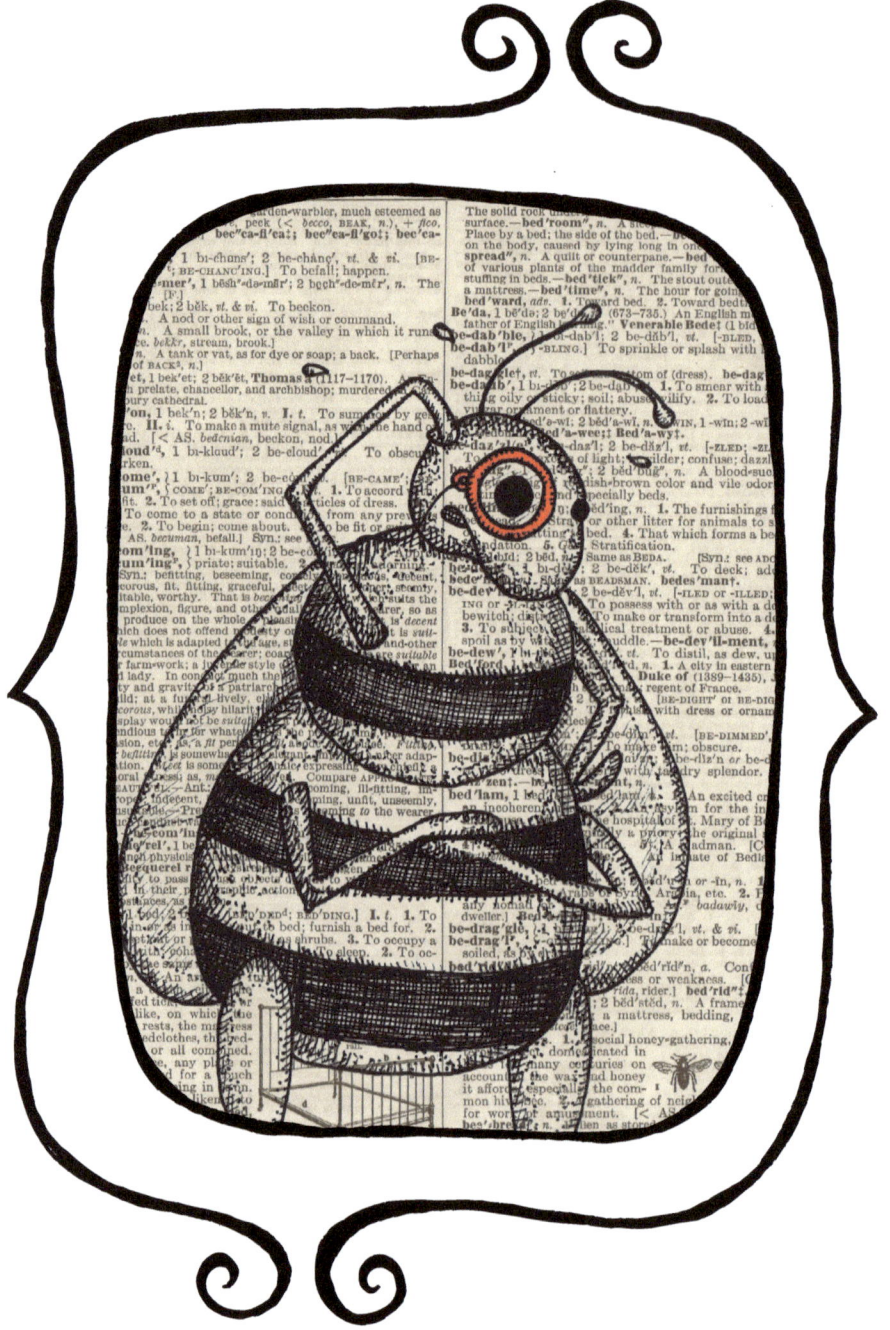

Meet Eugene the Bee

It's true that bees are hard workers, and Eugene's work ethic is only surpassed by his stress level. He worries about the future of bees, whether he left the oven on, and the mystery behind how a bee costume became a popular go-to for scantily-dressed girls on Halloween. Besides his tendency to fret, Eugene has also got a huge heart. He hopes this will one day be acknowledged by Mandi, the ladybug.

Meet Mandi the Ladybug

Mandi knows she's a ladybug living in man-bug's world. But Mandi is also smart enough to know that nothing can hold her back. Using her education, resources, and magnetism, Mandi acquired two hedges in the Hamptons as well as an Olive Tree condo before her pupa stage. She is a modern-day inspiration to many larvae out there.

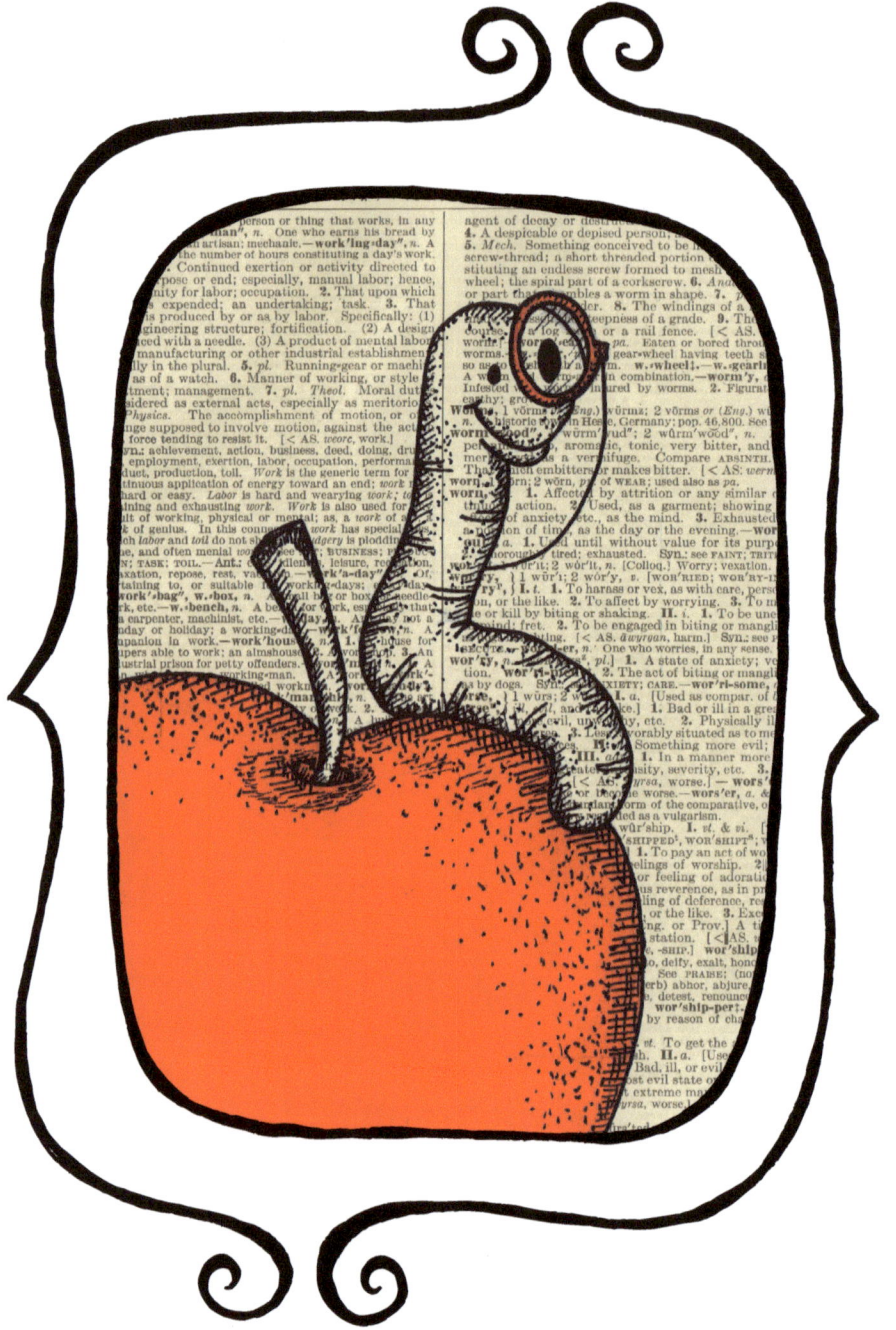

Meet Princeton the Inch Worm

Princeton is quite literally a book worm. He reads books. He discusses them. He eats them. Yes—Princeton does it all! He has seven doctorates ranging from parapsychology to philosophy. Ironically, Princeton is unemployed.

Meet Richard the Butterfly

Richard is a high-standing member in his community as well a several-time "Employee of the Month" at the Pollination Company. Despite his social and business obligations, Richard still manages to make time for his beautiful wife at home (not to mention 700 caterpillars on the way).

Meet Rufus the Anteater

Rufus may operate on a different standard of decorum, but that's how anteaters roll. When he is not dining in *Fear Factor* fashion, he is probably blowing your mind with some calculus. If you belong to a social circle that thinks "geeky is the new black" (like mathematicians, D&D enthusiasts, or hipsters), then you probably already know Rufus is legendary.

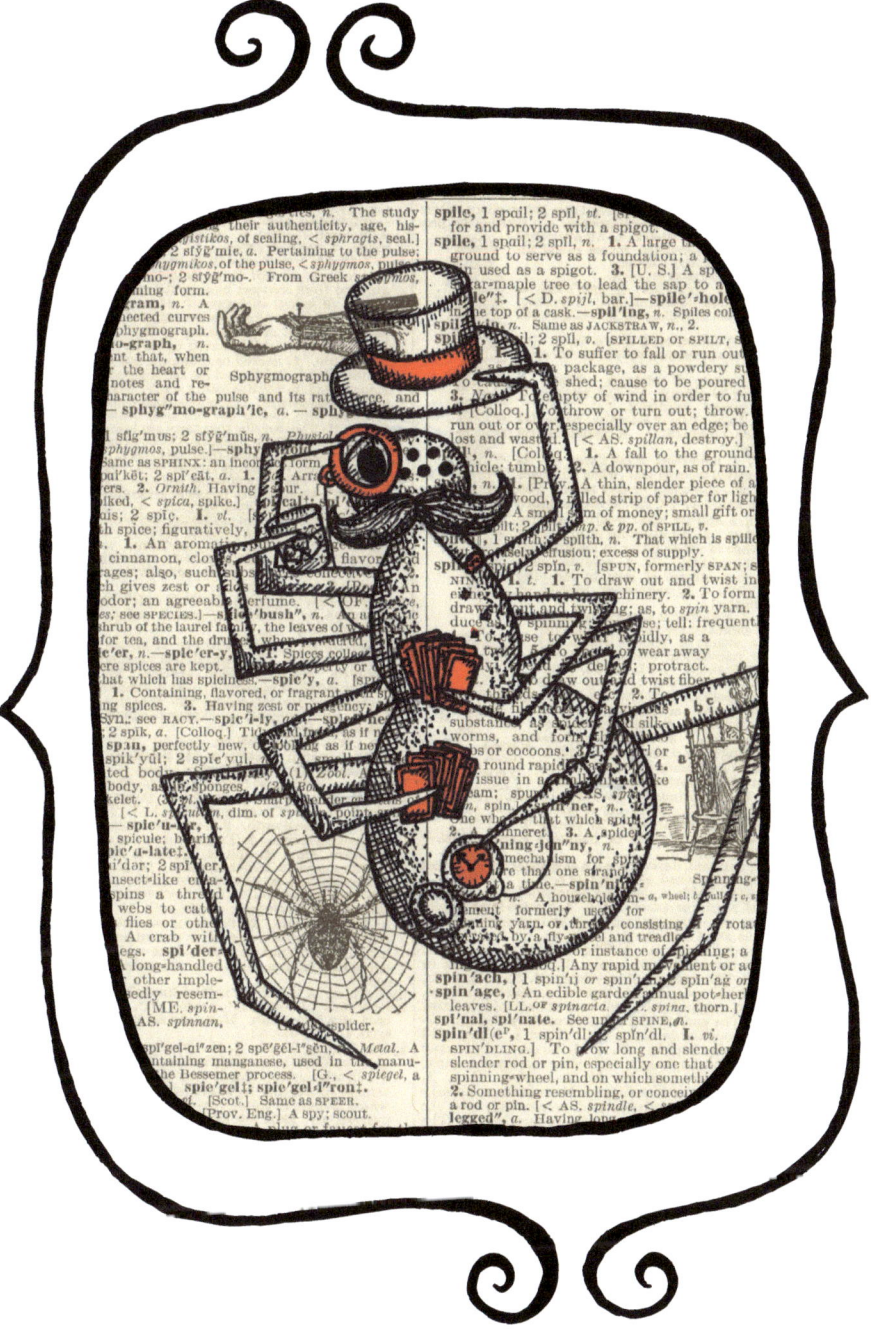

Meet Max the Spider

Whatever you can do, Max can do better and still have six arms left over. This is particularly true if the things you are doing are among his specialties, which include drinking, smoking, playing poker, and other indulgent practices. Surprisingly though, Max is only mediocre at making webs and catching bugs.

Meet Titch the Tiger

Titch is the life of any party as well as the highlight of any overnight drunk tank jail stay. Not that he seeks out trouble, it's just that this tiger's impromptu "dance-offs" often have unexpected consequences. Despite his occasional kerfuffle, Titch is one of the best fellas you'll ever meet. No matter where you are—corporate events, neighborhood bars, or jail—you're going to enjoy having him around.

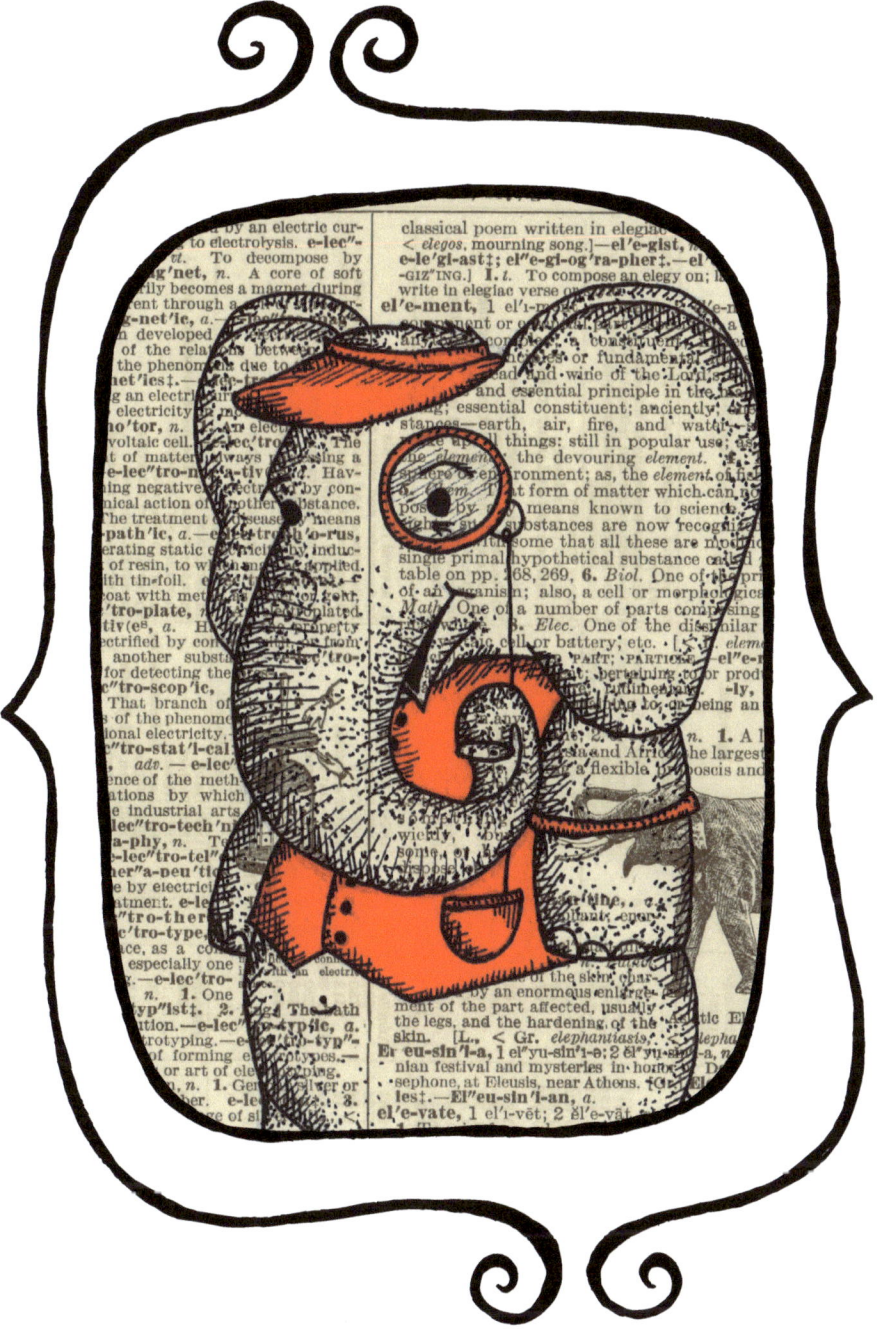

Meet Raymond the Elephant

Raymond is a very reliable and habitually punctual guy. In his uniform on the way to work, Raymond likes to pretend he's a no-nonsense, tough-guy bookie. Truth be known, he's actually a corporate accountant.

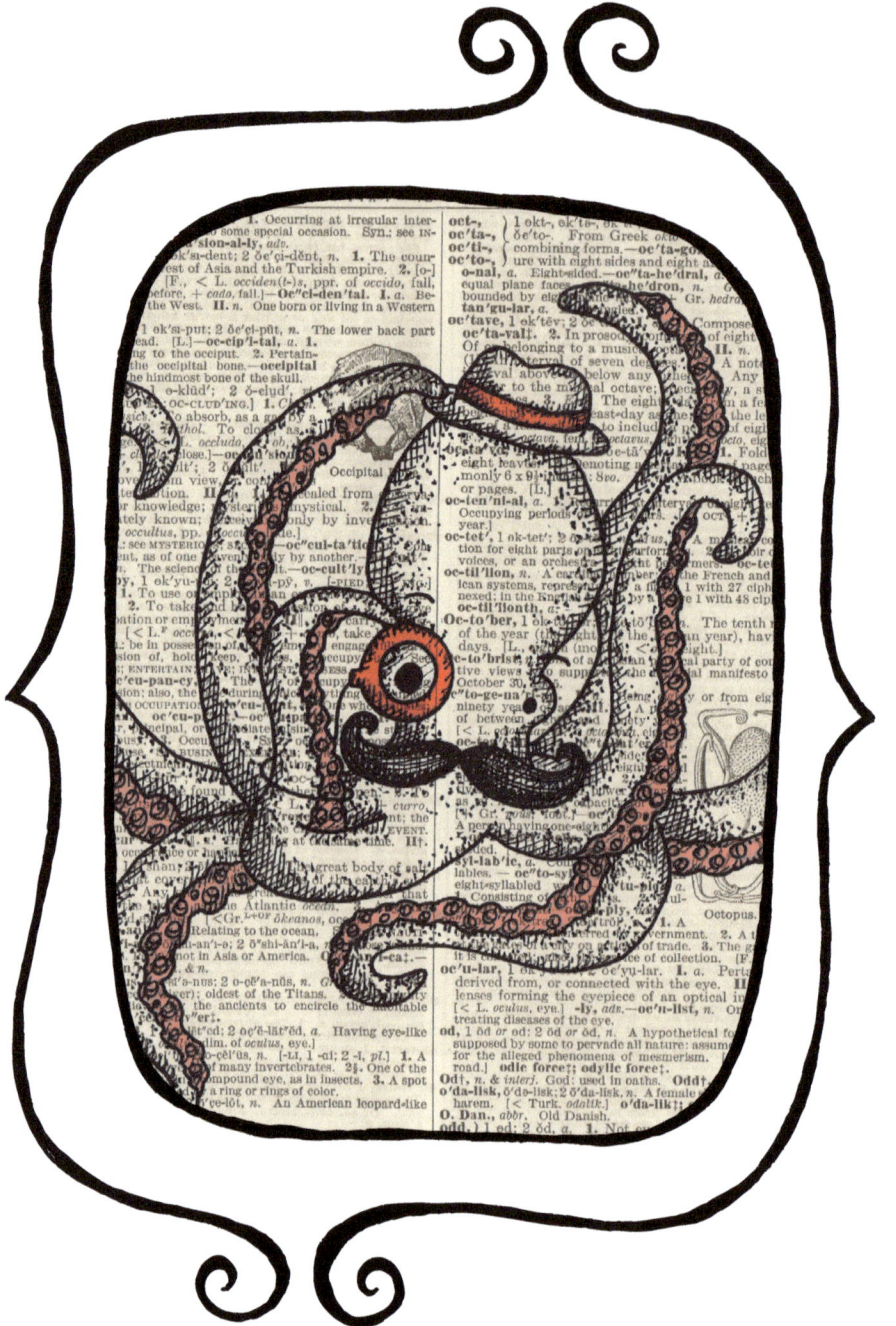

Meet Oscar the Octopus

The advantage of having eight arms is that you can be a very efficient multi-tasker. Oscar revels in this. Whether it's underwater welding, watercolor painting, or grooming his killer mustache, he can do it all at once with a few tentacles to spare. His versatile talents keep him very busy in life, although he still manages to make time for drumming in his Rush cover band.

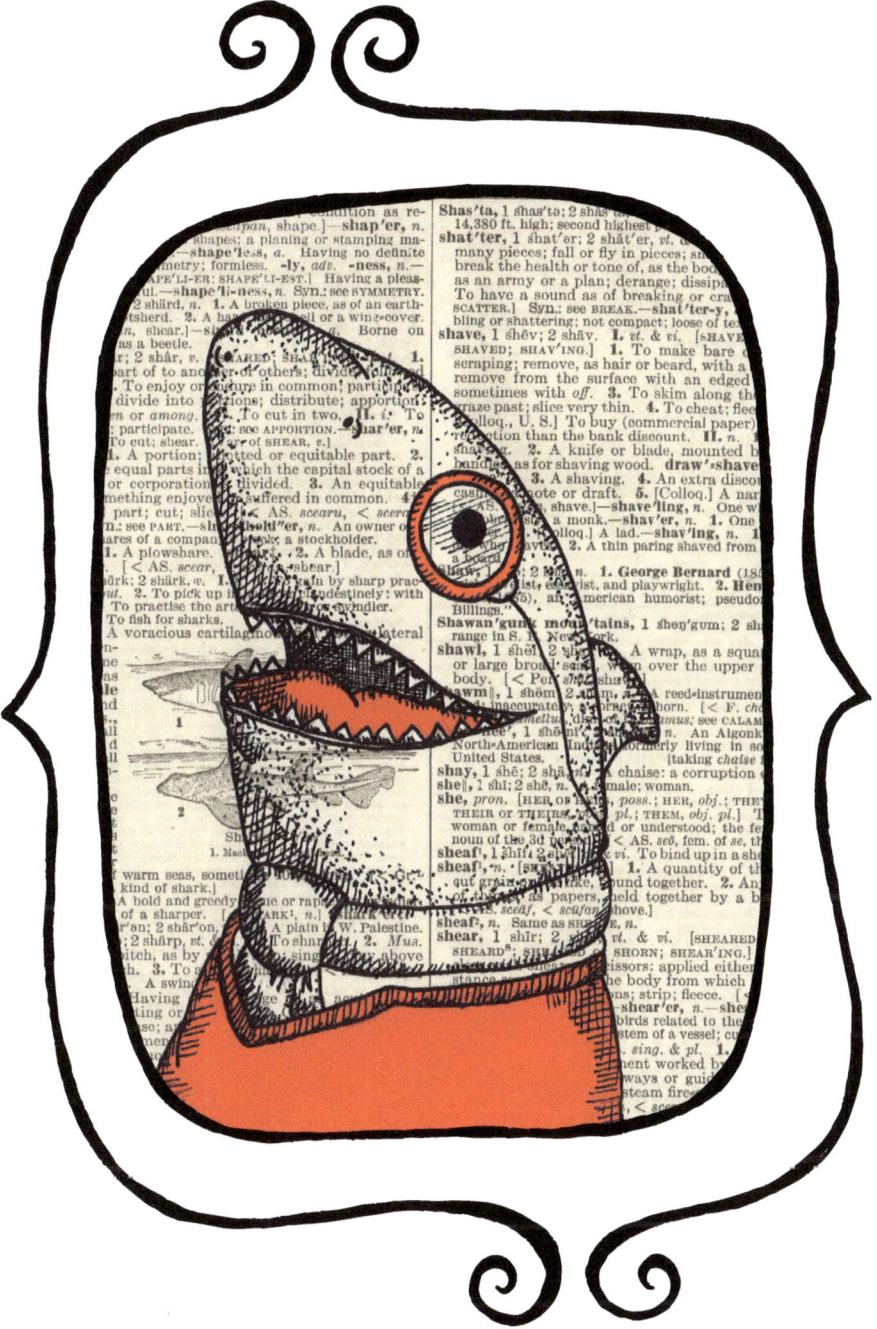

Meet Wally the Shark

Honestly, Wally is not the sharpest hook in the tackle box, but he comes from a prominent, affluent shark family and knows a lot of the "right" people. His proudest moment to date is a short cameo in the Syfy original film *Sharknado*. Wally can usually be found in his parents' basement, happily watching *Who's the Boss?* reruns.

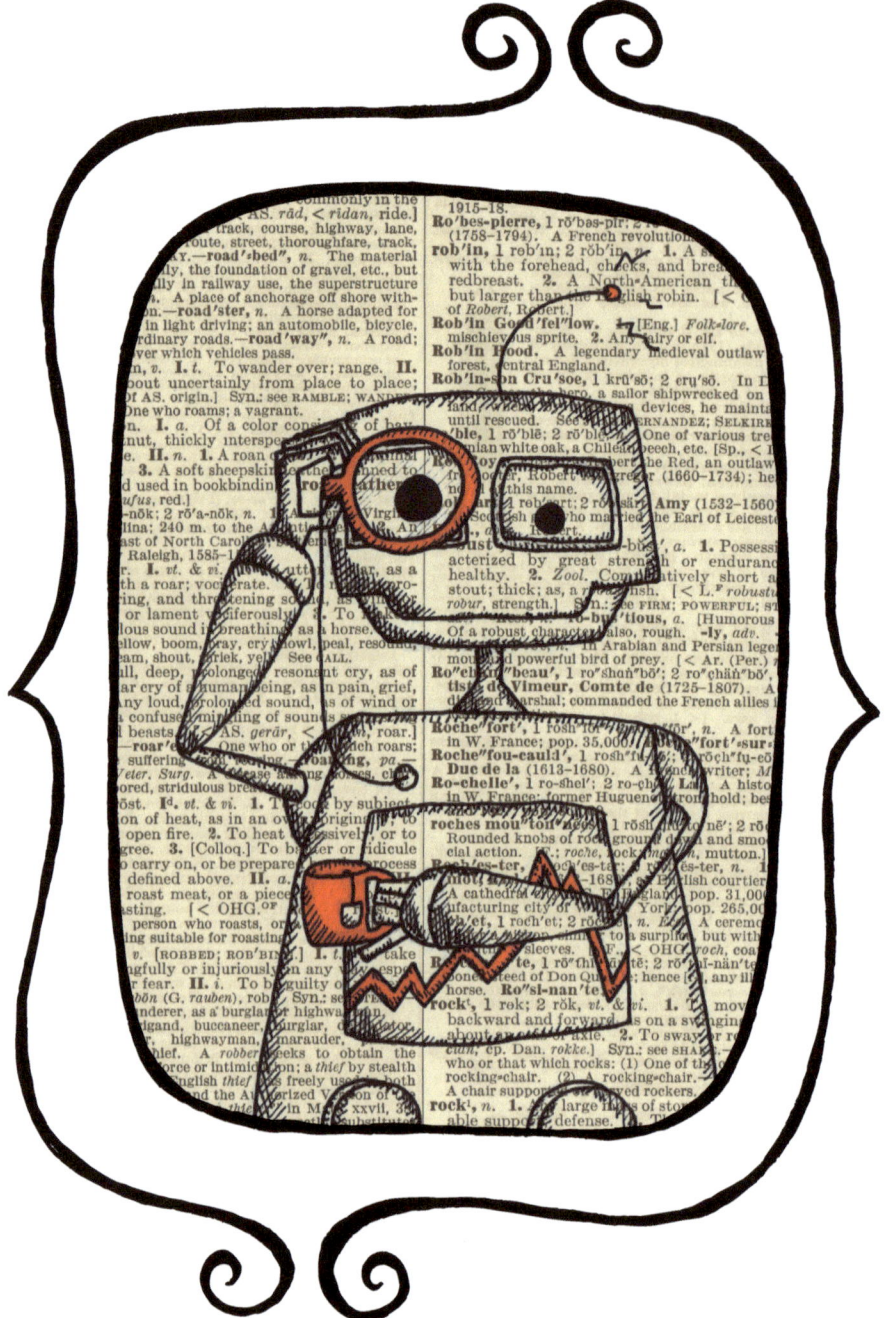

Meet Ralph 3000 the Robot

The Ralph 3000 is a very versatile friend. From yard work to taxes, he can help you with it all! In this particular shot, Ralph is in "pretentious mode" where he can be found wearing a monocle, sipping his tea, and correcting everyone's grammar.

Meet Don and Joey

This renaissance Kangaroo is both a lover and a fighter. His varied skill sets keep him highly revered throughout the Outback, but no one looks up to him more than his little sidekick, Joey.

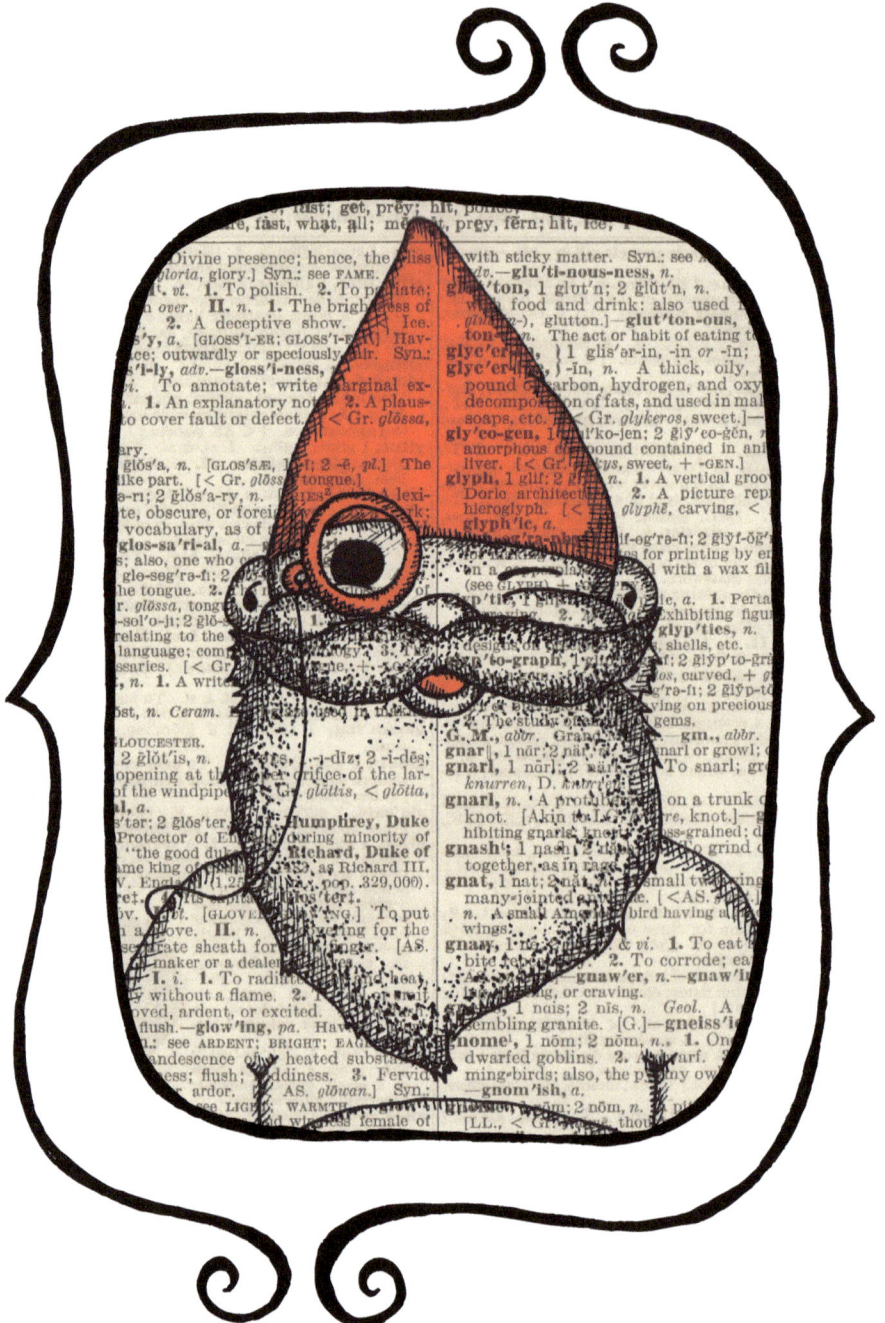

Meet Nolan the Gnome

Nolan is no "one-trick gnomey." Though you might find him smoking a pipe in the shrubs or hanging out with a mushroom in the back yard, don't let Nolan's adorable manner mislead you. He is a soldier who will defend your garden at any cost. Sleep safely knowing Nolan is on your lawn's side.

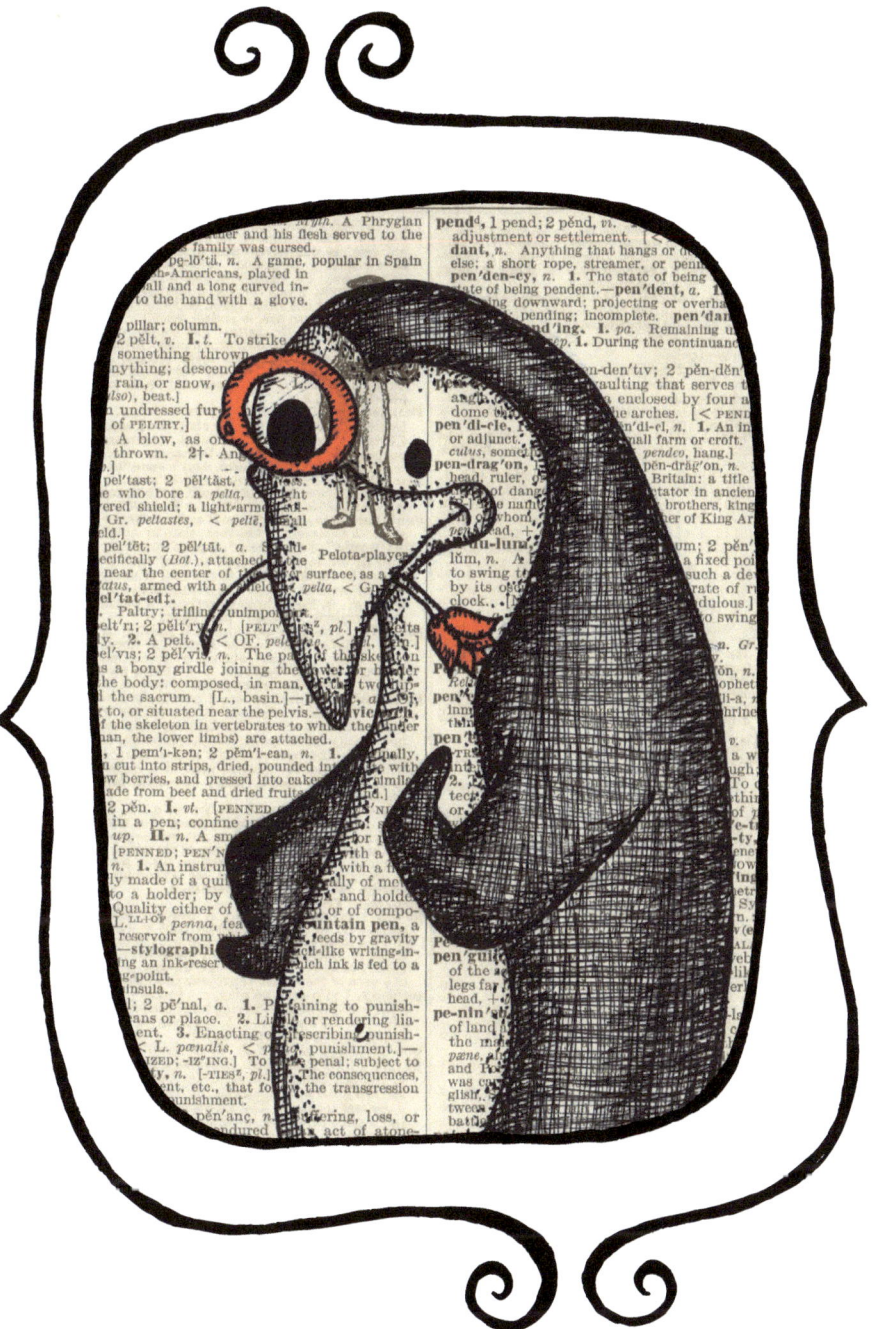

Meet Jules the Penguin

With a natural widow's peak and a permanent tuxedo, Jules rocks the monocle like nobody else. His innate wit and solid dance moves drive the girls wild. It's not surprising that female penguins decide to mate for life.

Meet Godzilla and Mothra

How do you remain two of the most epic villains in history? You have to keep up with the times! In our modern world, Godzilla and Mothra realize that it's not always about surprise attacks and brute force. Sometimes you just need to hash out conflict over a cup of tea and polite discussion. Their new tactics lead to less exciting movie plots, but many city-dwellers thank them.

Meet Clarence the Angler Fish

When your body is designed for the bottom of the sea, you may not be considered conventionally attractive. Luckily, Clarence is the type of fish who knows he must rely on other strengths, like taste and humor. You might see him fashionably accessorizing with a monocle or hat. During Christmas season, Clarence has been known to wrap mistletoe on his lure. His philosophy is, "If you can't have a good time while tempting fish into a death trap, then why live?" Clarence may be slightly sociopathic.

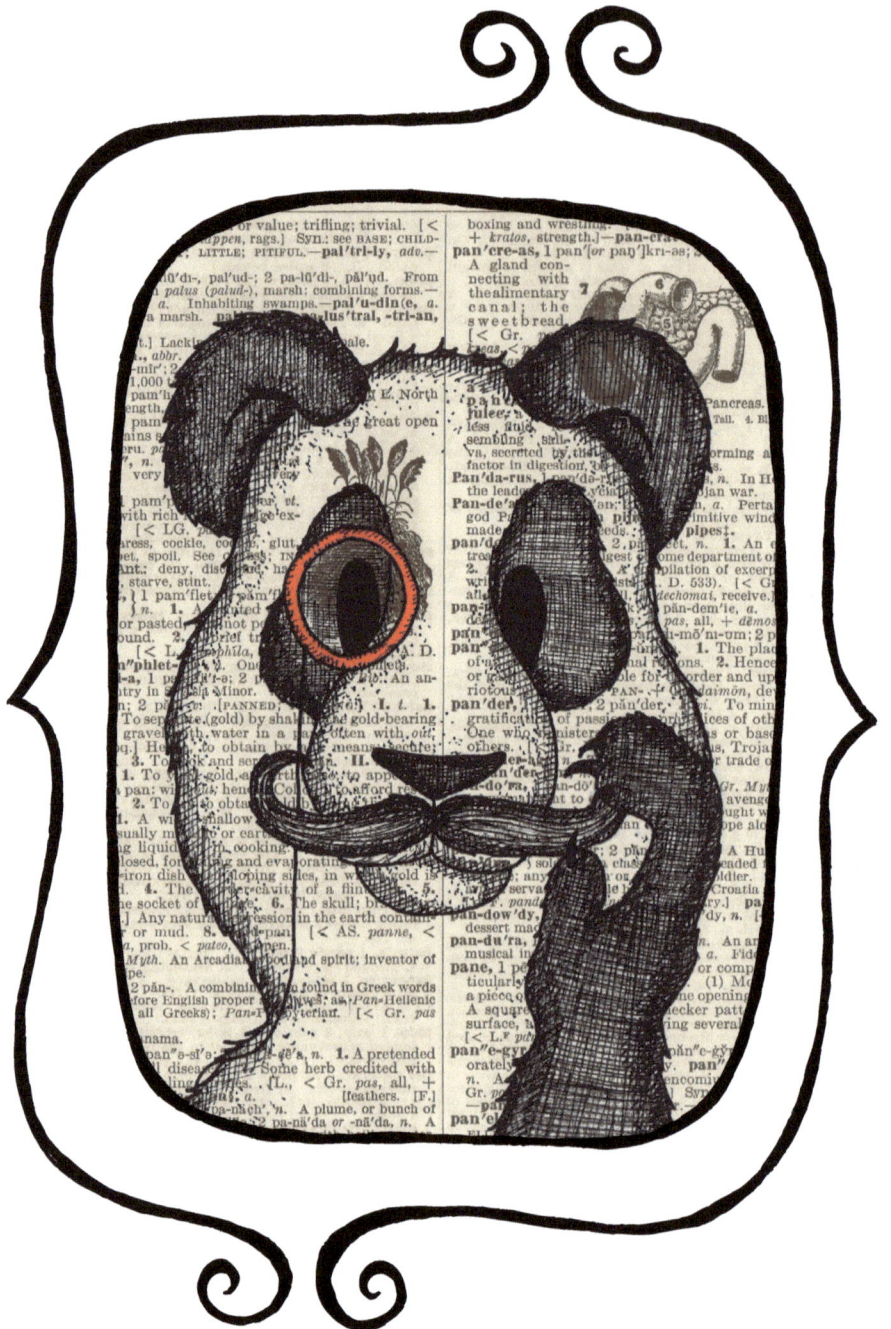

Meet Lincoln the Panda

Lincoln is 20% cute, 20% intellectual, and 60% wild card. One minute you might be discussing the American classics, while the next, he's killed half your family because his blood sugar was a little low. Somehow, though, you'll find yourself drawn to Lincoln in the same way that guys dig crazy chicks—because he's just pretty enough to pull it off.

Meet Tom the Polar Bear

Dressed to the nines in his bowler hat, Tom thinks there is no reason to forgo your sense of fashion just because you swim and kill all day. He's kind of like the Jason Statham of the Arctic.

Meet Gordon and Cody

Gordon the hippo and his little friend, Cody, have a symbiotic relationship. Cody cleans the bugs off Gordon's back and packs his pipe, while Gordon agrees not to roll over in his sleep and crush Cody. And that, my friends, is how timeless friendships are born.

Meet Rupert the Manatee

Despite an extreme lack of work as a struggling actor, Rupert the Manatee has an optimism that is contagious. He is stuck in the purgatory of not being ugly enough for the typecast walrus roles, while not being svelte enough to score the leading seal parts. In between auditions, Rupert keeps his head held high, seeking free food where he can find it and knowing his big break is coming soon.

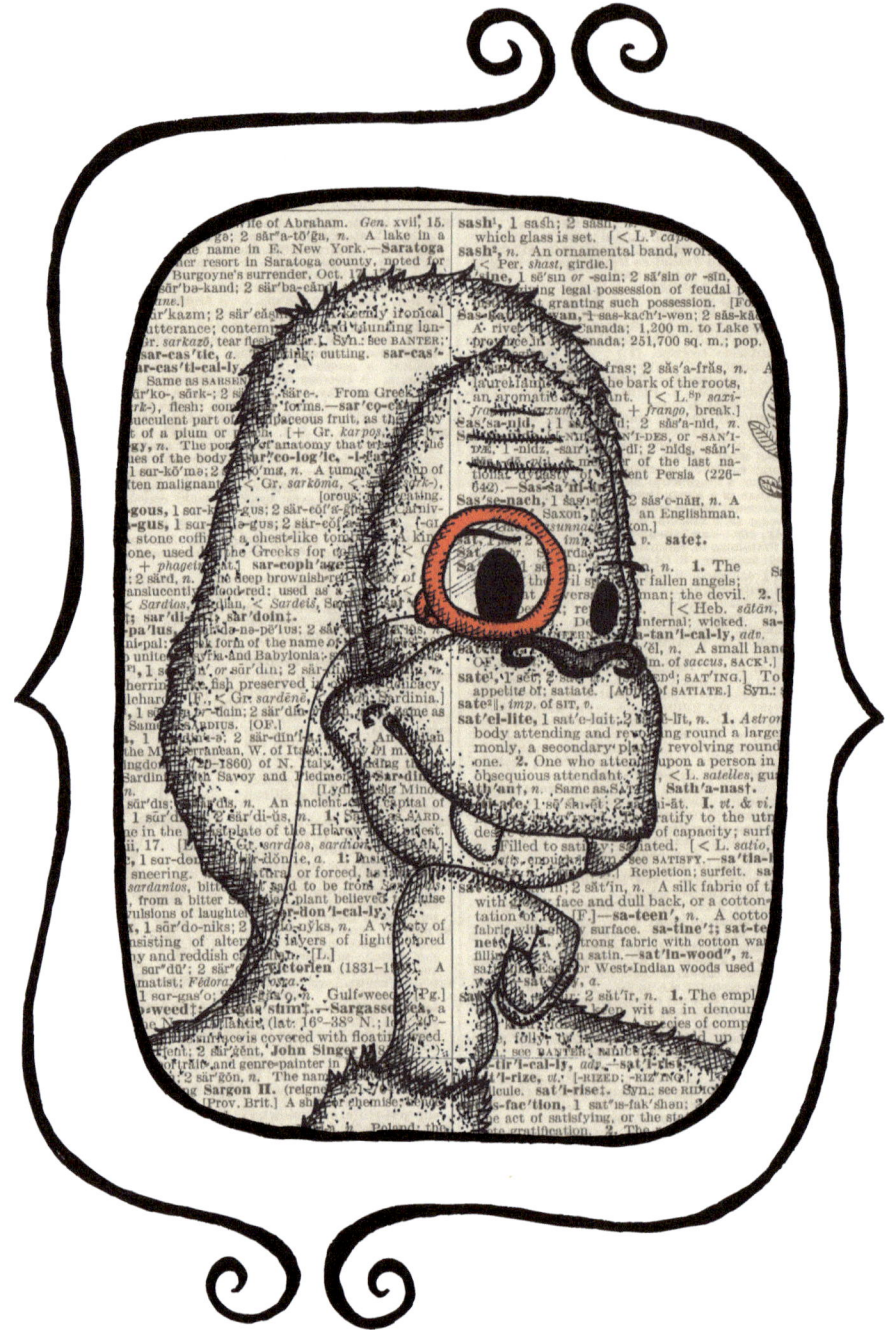

Meet Barry the Sasquatch

Barry is astonishingly poised and always ready for a glamour shot. For decades, he's been single-handedly trying to change the mindset of his stubborn fellow Sasquatch. Barry has had enough of hiding in the woods, with only pixelated images and a few poor quality videos to show for it. He plans to be the face of the new, rebranded, public Big Foot! Given the rise in popularity of facial hair, Barry thinks there is no time like the present. He can be found on all social networks but has yet to be taken very seriously.

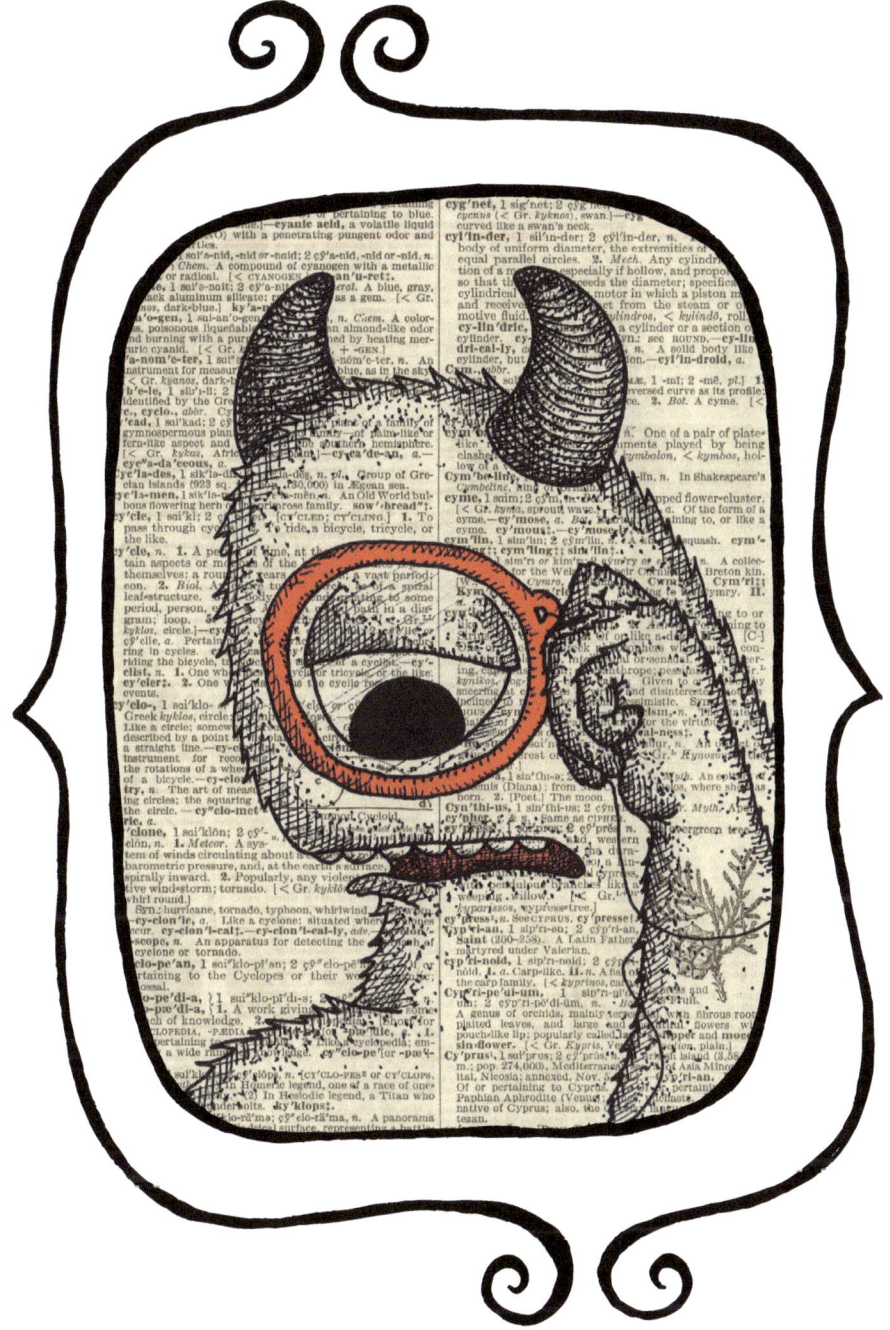

Meet Wiploc the Cyclops

Growing up as a visually impaired Cyclops, Wiploc had a tough childhood. Names like "Ol' Two-Eyes" can really stick with you. Despite his rough start, Wiploc conquered adversity by using his experiences to inspire the start of many Cyclops' awareness and tolerance groups. He is presently trying to get Homer's *Odyssey* banned from public libraries. Wiploc remains optimistic, though he has had no success to date.

Meet Cheez Whiz the Pug

It's hard to gain respect at high-class charity functions when your name tag reads "Cheez Whiz," but don't be misled. Just because he might have eaten squeeze cheese as a puppy doesn't mean he won't be the first to tell you if your foie gras is less than stellar.

Meet Magnum the Dog

While a dog of his stature weighs only about six pounds, this salty sea captain unequivocally commands the respect of his entire crew. Others in his position might have come to power through brute force, but that isn't Magnum's style. He knows that it's much easier to reel everyone in with cuteness…and then outsmart them all.

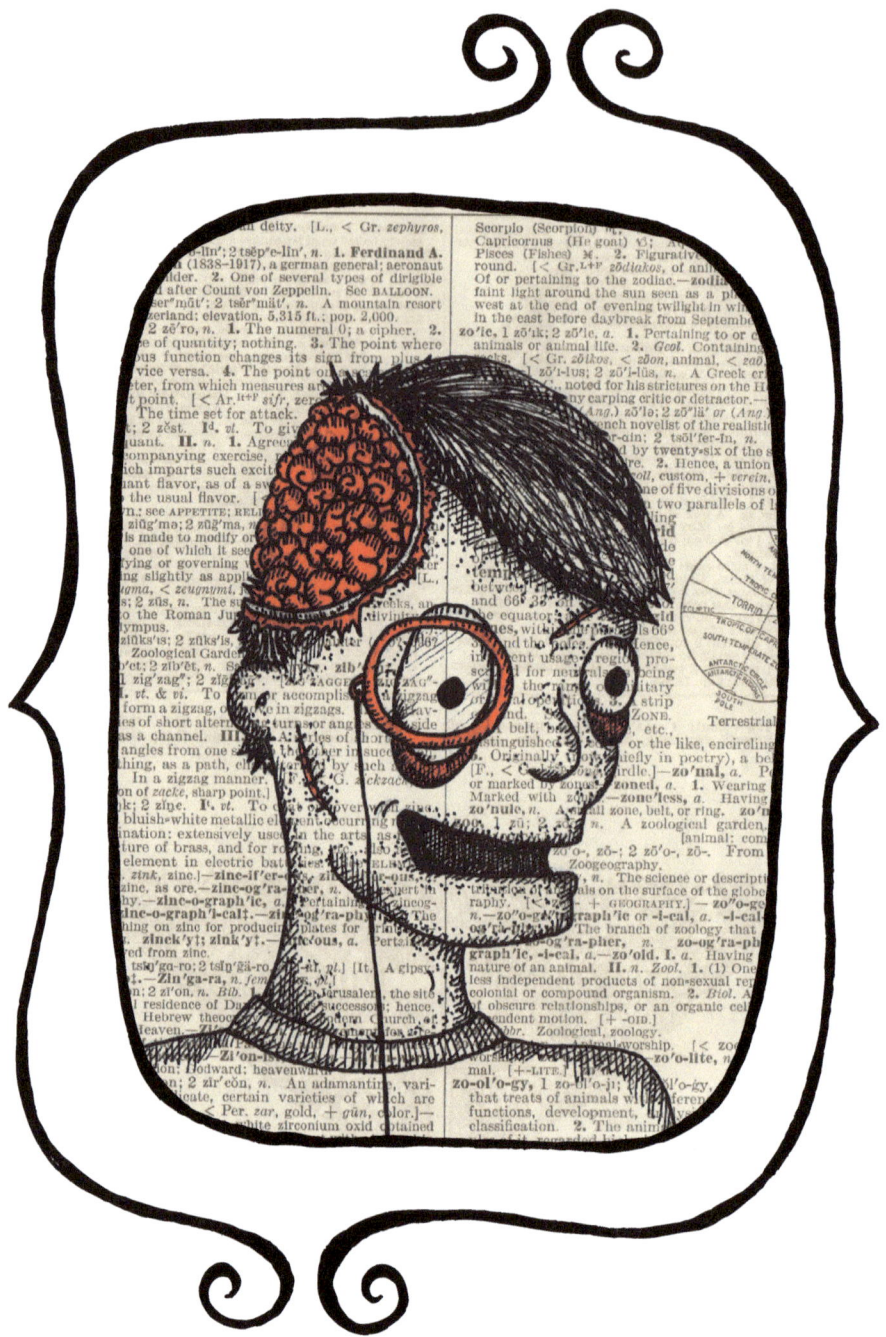

Meet Zeke the Zombie

Zeke was a trendsetter in life and continues to be one after death. At first glance, he may seem to be little more than a bag of rotting flesh. "That may be true," he insists, "but it doesn't mean I can't keep it classy." Zeke can often be spotted at AMC red carpet events.

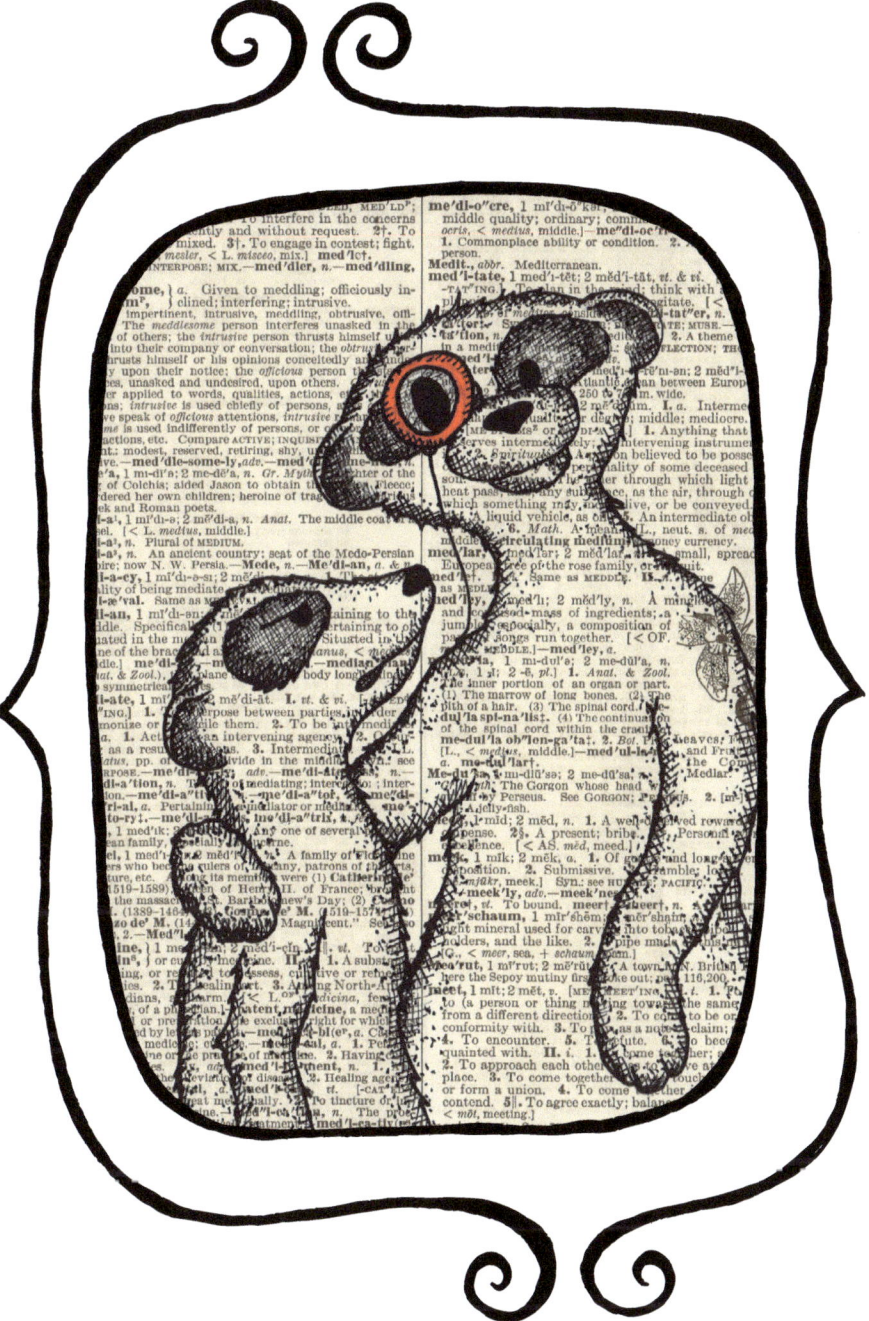

Meet Frick and Frack

Times can be tough at Meerkat Manor with over fifty mouths to feed and only one monocle to go around. Frick, the oldest, is quick to take advantage of his seniority. Of course, anyone with an older sibling can empathize with Frack, understanding that his time is evenly split between hero worship and sheer contempt.

Meet Alfie the Goat

With a tin can in one hoof and a master's degree in the other, Alfie is a walking goat paradox. While a lesser man may judge Alfie for his abnormal culinary preferences, most commend him. Alfie might be a Harvard goat, but he finds it important to remember one's roots.

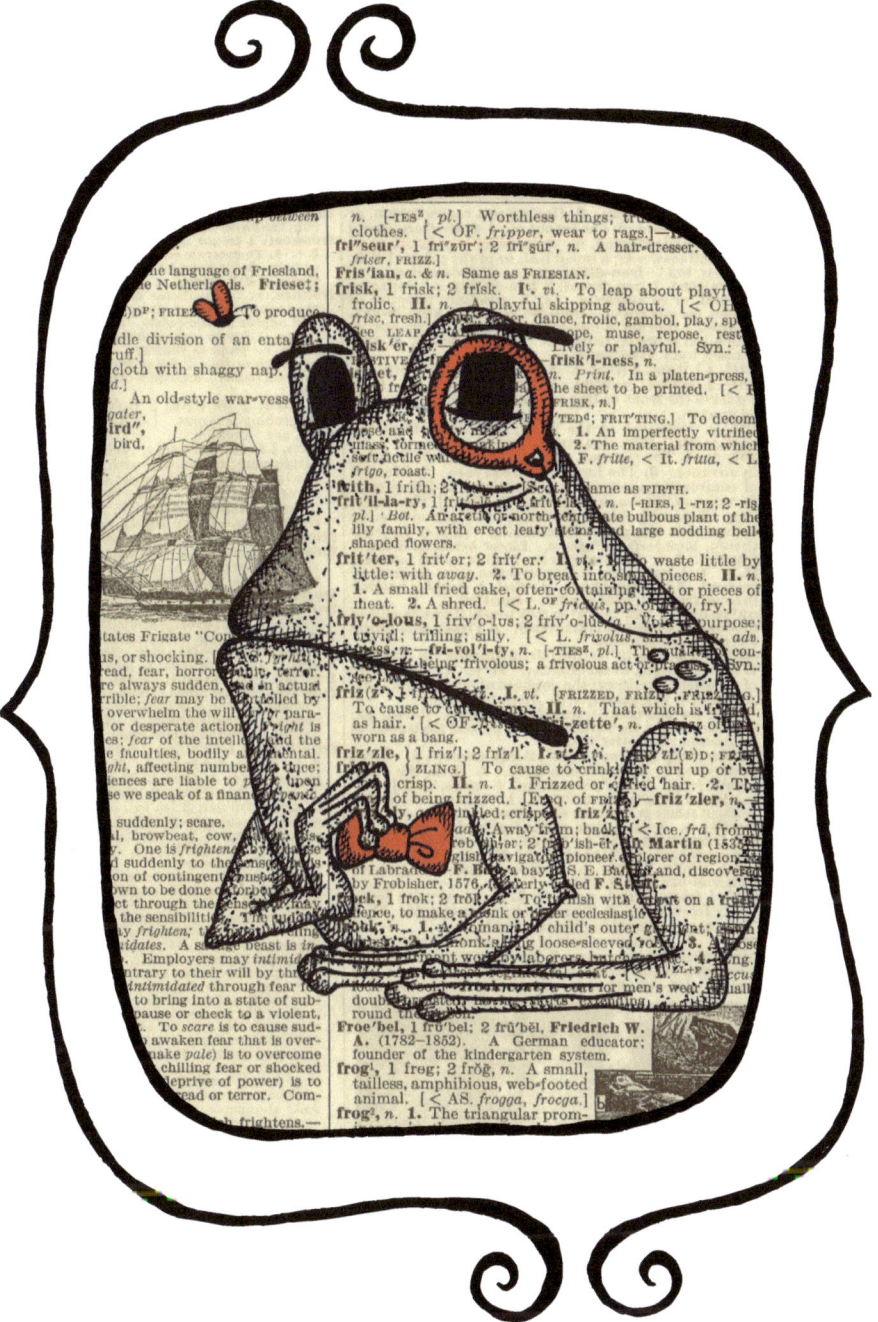

Meet Vernon the Frog

Vernon considers being "snooty" part of a frog's natural instincts. He sticks to a strict diet of escargot and caviar, and you will never get a glimpse of Vernon catching food with his tongue. He deems this unsophisticated and claims that any evidence you might have seen of such an event is fabricated by the liberal toad media.

Meet Archie Prickles the Hedgehog

As a hedgehog, Archie understands the curse of being adorable. It's hard to be taken seriously at the office when everyone just wants to rub his belly. Archie strives to be as productive as possible, but he also takes solace in the thought, "Who could actually fire a face like this?" Archie excels at monthly time audits, work Christmas parties, and water cooler conversation.

Meet Tami Boyce the Author/Illustrator

"A LOVE FOR DRAWING has been present in my life for as long as I can remember. I consider myself lucky to be able to incorporate what I love into what I do.

It took me a long time to trust my gut when it came to my illustration style. After all, the art world can be a very serious and competitive place. But one day I realized that while there are already plenty of artists who offer beautiful sunset paintings to the world, there's really only one who is making sure the world has enough illustrations of llamas on bikes and narwhals holding balloons.

That would be me.

I pull inspiration for my art from both my humor and my heart. Some of my illustrations are observations on life, some are memories, and some are wishful thinking as to how animals might actually behave in the wild.

The Monocle Series is very close to my heart, not just because it was so incredibly fun to draw, but it was also one of my first set of drawings which gave me the confidence to pursue illustration professionally.

Over the years, it has been awesome to see people enjoy these monocled characters as art prints. This book marks the first time the entire gang appears along with their bios as a complete collection!"

Tami Boyce is a Charleston-based illustrator and graphic designer. Her work can be found at various establishments around Charleston, South Carolina, including Theatre 99, Early Bird Diner, Frothy Beard Brewery, ReForm Studios, as well as in ZaPow! Gallery in Asheville, NC. To see more of her work, please visit tamiboyce.com.

Photograph by Leslie McKellar (www.leslieryannmckellar.com)

www.ingramcontent.com/pod-product-compliance
Lightning Source LLC
Chambersburg PA
CBHW041933180426
43198CB00033B/103